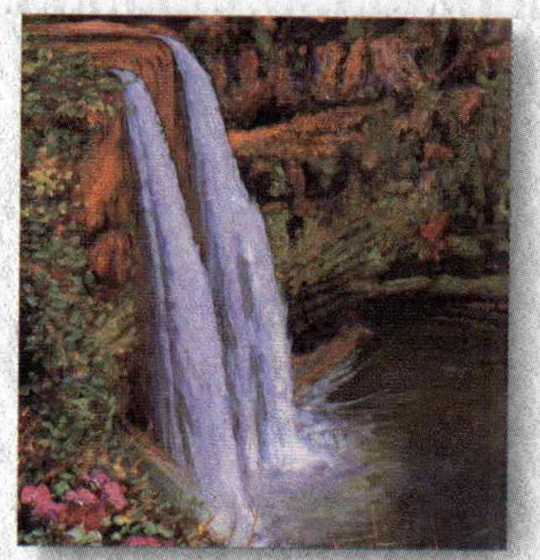

Scenes
Around the World

Acrylic paints are probably more fun and easier to control than any other medium I've worked in. A forgiving medium—especially if you're just starting out—acrylic has quick-drying properties that allow you to paint over areas of your work without delay. And the various acrylic mediums available offer a wide range of possible modifications—such as slowing the drying time, thinning the paints, or building up texture—allowing you to create a variety of effects. All this makes acrylic ideal for depicting subjects and scenes from around the world, with their wide diversity of texture and color. Combine these advantages with the fact that acrylic also cleans up easily with soap and water, and it's hard to argue against acrylic as a painting medium! I hope you enjoy the experience of working with acrylic as you paint the scenes featured in this book. From a lush, tropical Hawaiian waterfall and a warm Mediterranean sunset to an old-world landmark and a busy European street scene—with acrylic, you can capture it all. —*Tom Swimm*

CONTENTS

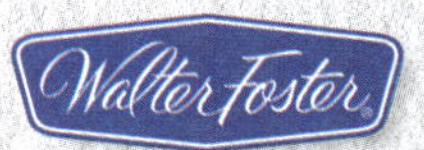

CHOOSING TOOLS AND MATERIALS

To get started with acrylic, all you need are a few basic tools: paints, brushes, supports, and water. The supplies are not only minimal, they're also easy to come by; all these materials are readily available at any local art store. You won't need any solvents or harsh chemicals to work in acrylic—the wet paint can be thinned with plain water, and brushes can be cleaned with any mild, soapy solution. Acrylic can also be mixed with many different painting mediums to change its consistency. (See page 3.) Here you'll find an overview of the acrylic tools and materials; for a more in-depth description, refer to *Watercolor & Acrylic Painting Materials* by William F. Powell in the Artist's Library Series.

SELECTING PAINTS

Acrylic paints come in jars, cans, and tubes. Most artists prefer tubes, as they make it easy to squeeze out the appropriate amount of paint onto your palette. There are two types of paints available: "student grade" and more expensive "artist grade." Artist-grade paints contain more pigment and fewer fillers, so they are more vibrant and produce richer mixes. When you purchase paints—or any acrylic supplies—remember to buy the best you can afford at the time, as better quality materials are more manageable and also produce longer-lasting works.

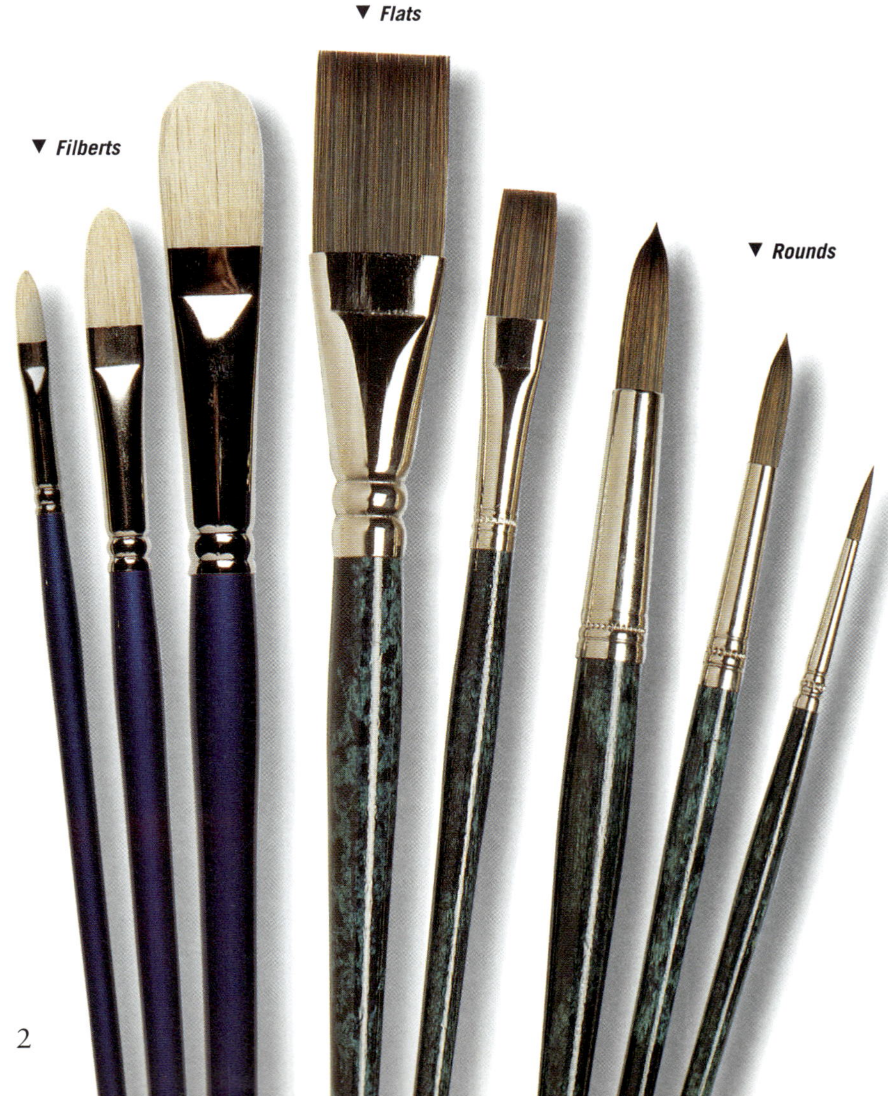

▼ *Flats*

▼ *Filberts*

▼ *Rounds*

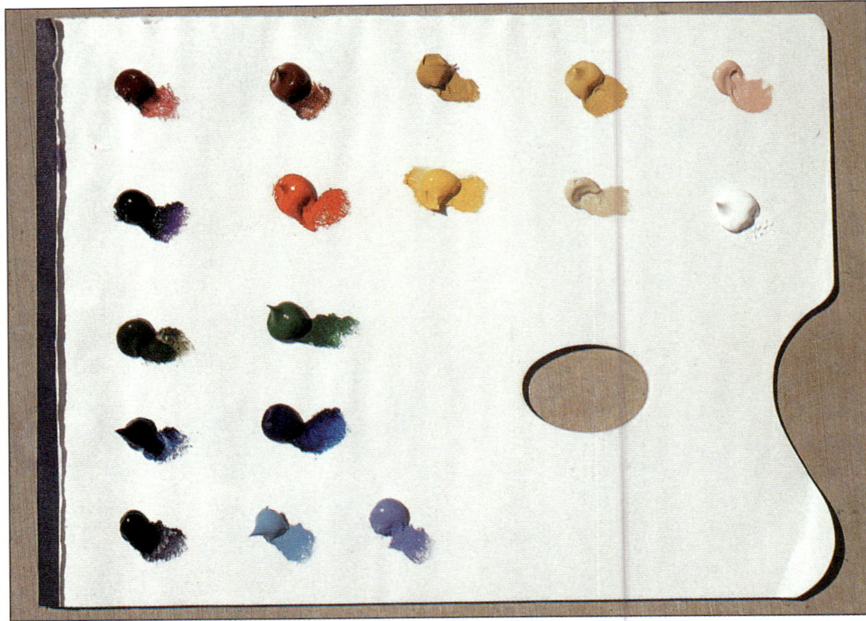

DETERMINING A PALETTE A good basic color palette usually includes one warm and one cool version of each primary color (red, blue, and yellow). My basic palette consists of (from the top, moving left to right): alizarin crimson, burnt sienna, yellow ochre, Naples yellow, light portrait pink, dioxazine purple, cadmium red light, cadmium yellow light, unbleached titanium, titanium white, sap green, emerald green, Prussian blue, phthalo blue, Payne's gray, cerulean blue, and light blue-violet.

DRAWING WITH THE BRUSH

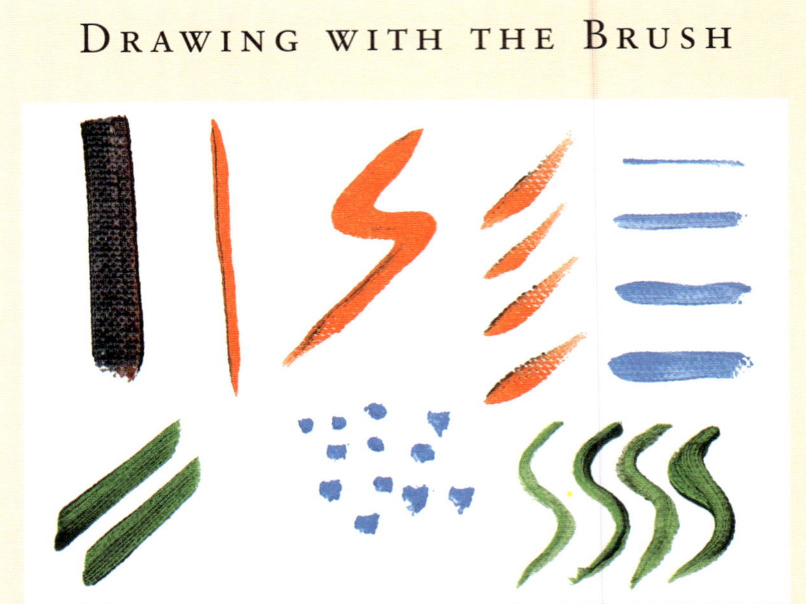

PRACTICING "DRAWING" You can use the tip of a filbert or a round brush to make long, thin lines or even small dots. And a flat brush can produce thicker lines or, when turned on its edge, thin, crisp lines. Practice "drawing" with your brushes at various angles to see the kinds of lines you can create.

BUYING BRUSHES

Acrylic paintbrushes are categorized by hair type (soft or stiff and natural or synthetic), style (filbert, flat, or round), and size. For the projects in this book, I recommend small, medium, and large sizes of both soft and stiff brushes. Synthetic-hair brushes work well with acrylic, as the bristles are soft but springy enough to return to their original form. Flat brushes are good for producing straight, sharp edges or filling large areas of color. And small round and filbert brushes have pointed tips that are well suited for details.

◄ BRUSH BASICS Some brushes are sized by inches, and others are sized by number. A universal standard for brush sizes doesn't exist, so sizes will vary slightly from manufacturer to manufacturer; but typically larger numbers are applied to bigger brushes. Buy brushes that are appropriate for the size of work you'll be creating, and be sure to have a variety of smaller brushes on hand for "drawing" details. (See "Drawing with the Brush" above.)

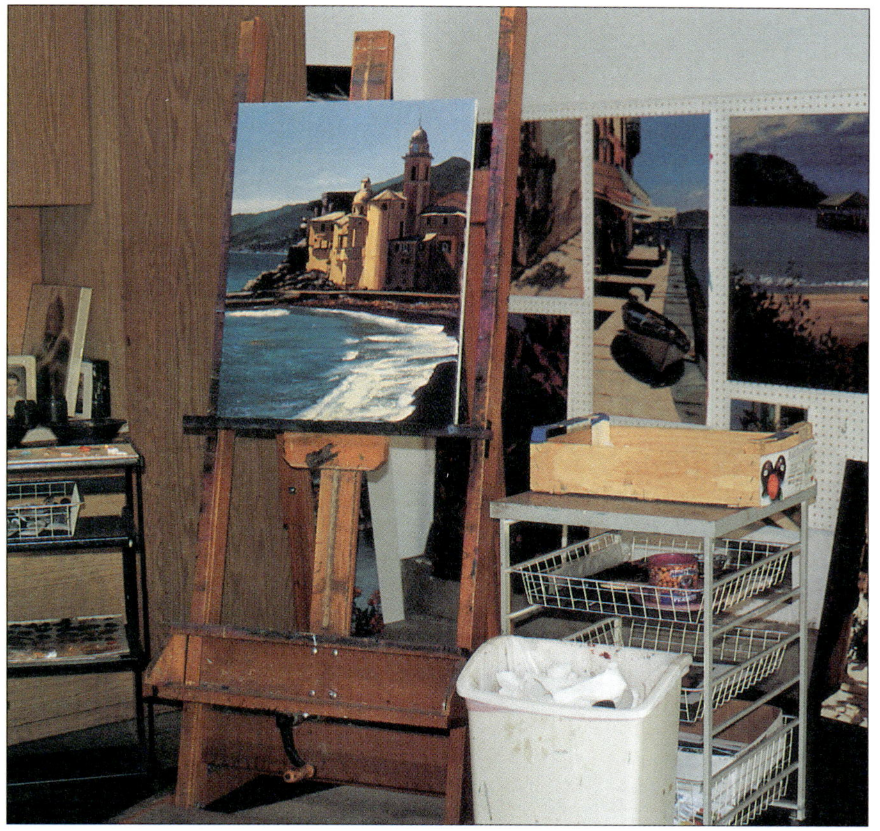

SETTING UP A WORK SPACE When establishing your work space, choose a location with plenty of lighting where you can keep your tools and materials within easy reach. A studio can be located anywhere—from your home office to your kitchen table. My studio is located inside my garage! With the garage door open, my workspace gets plenty of natural northern light, and I also have an overhead array of track lighting so that I can work at night. Next to my easel, I set up a multi-level artist's taboret to keep my tools close at hand. And on the wall, I keep a pegboard for hanging works in progress as they dry.

MEDIUMS

Water is not the only substance that you can add to your acrylic paint to alter its consistency. There are a variety of acrylic mediums you can use to achieve various effects—from thin, glossy layers to thick, impasto strokes. In the projects in this book, I use only a few mediums, but it's a good idea to get to know all the possibilities.

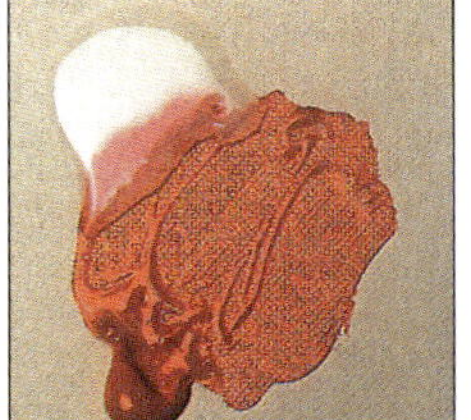

Gloss medium

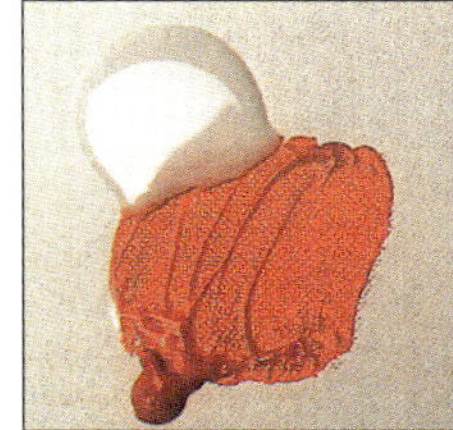

Matte medium

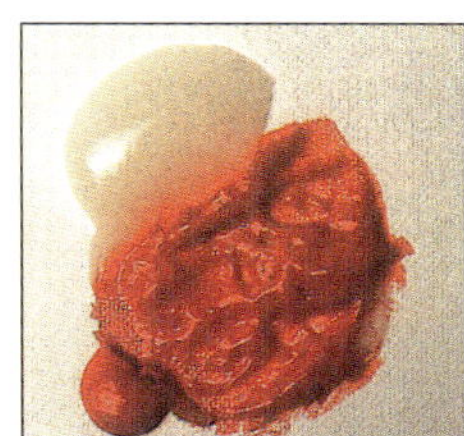

Gel medium

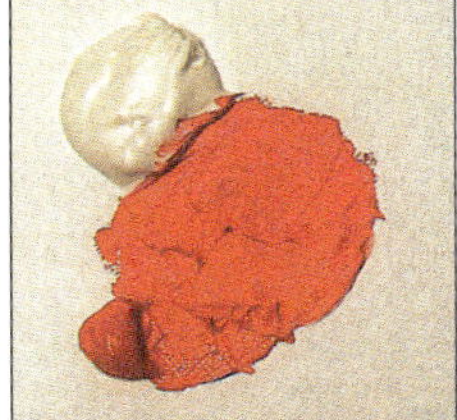

Texture medium

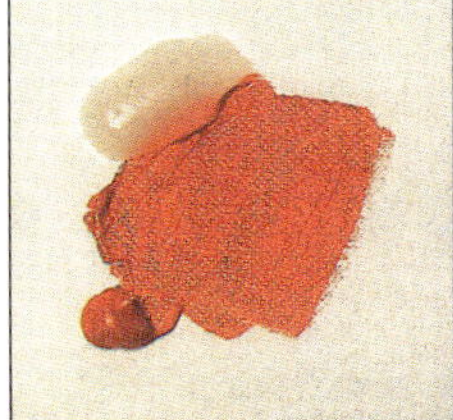

Retarding medium

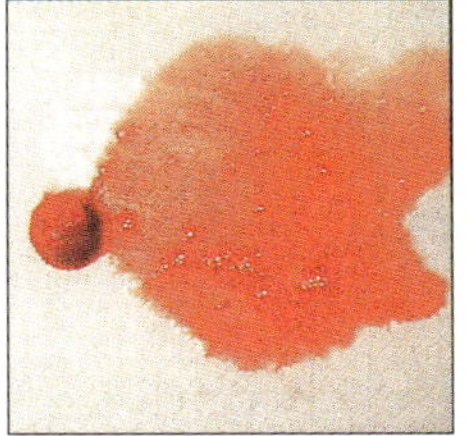

Flow improver

UNDERSTANDING MEDIUMS *Gloss* medium is a runny fluid that is useful for thinning the paint while maintaining its luster. In contrast, *matte* medium causes the paint to dry to a soft sheen. (*Satin* medium—not pictured—produces a similar effect.) *Gel* medium has more body than gloss or matte mediums, giving the paint a heavier consistency for thick strokes. *Texture* mediums are even thicker, and they come in different types, such as sand and fiber. *Retarding* medium helps slow the drying time of the paints. And *flow improver* increases the fluidity of paint and eliminates brush marks within strokes. Although these mediums may at first appear milky or opaque, most dry clear or almost clear.

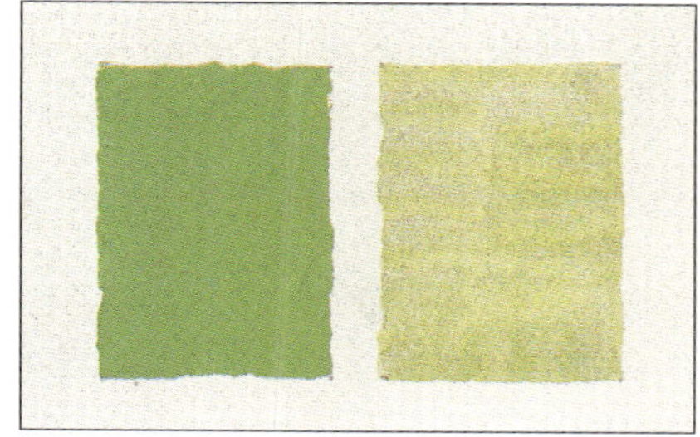

Canvas

Illustration board

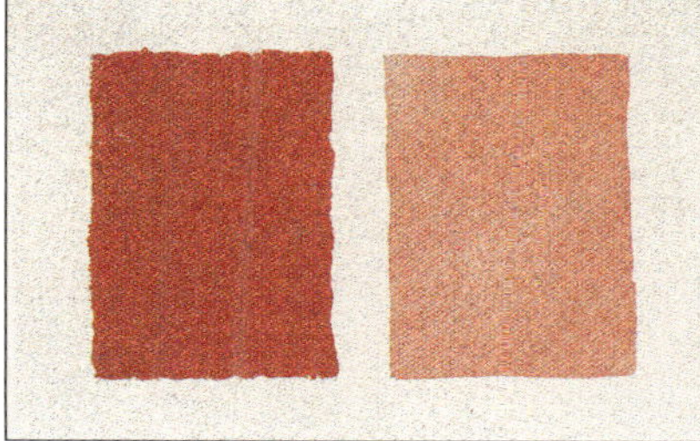

Primed hardwood panel (smooth side)

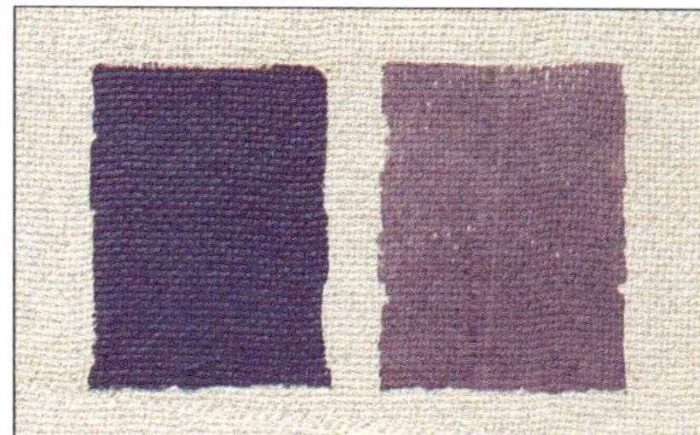

Primed hardwood panel (rough side)

CHOOSING A PAINTING SURFACE Many acrylic artists paint on primed canvas or canvas board which has a clothlike grain. Illustration board and primed pressed-wood panels are other good choices. Each type of support has a different surface texture that affects the way it accepts paint. Above you can see how four common painting surfaces accept thick applications (left) and thin applications (right).

SELECTING A PALETTE

There is no "standard" mixing palette for acrylic paints, and artists often experiment with a few different types before finding one that works best for them. And acrylic painters have many palette options—porcelain, plexiglass, plastic, plate glass, or any other non-porous, nonabsorbent material will do. Some artists use disposable waxed-paper palettes, but there are no barriers along the edges to keep large amounts of wet paint on the palette and they make it difficult to keep the paints damp. Because it's important to keep acrylic paints moist, many artists place a wet paper towel underneath the paints, spritzing the paints with a water bottle or adding retarder to the paints (see "Mediums" at left) to keep them from drying.

GATHERING A FEW "EXTRAS"

In addition to brushes, paints, a palette, and supports, you'll also want to keep a few other supplies on hand as you paint. Palette knives and painting knives are great for mixing colors or applying thick paint to the canvas. A roll of paper towels will come in handy for keeping your brushes and your painting area clean. And jars of fresh water are also important; designate one for rinsing your brushes and one for adding pure water to your color mixes. To make sure your paints stay moist, keep a spray bottle full of water near your palette. And it's always useful to have drawing tools nearby!

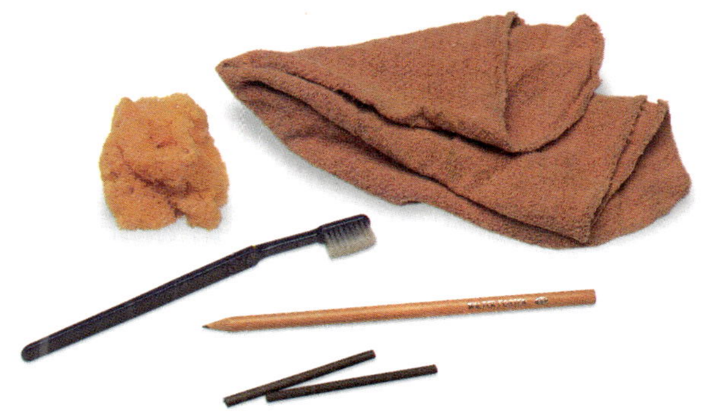

◄ ADDING SUPPLIES As an artist, I've learned to be prepared for just about anything while painting! I use drawing tools—such as pencils, charcoal, or markers—to sketch on my support, and I always have a rag close at hand for quick and easy cleanup. Toothbrushes, sponges, and other household items are also great for creating textures!

FOCUSING ON COMPOSITION

Composition is an important element of any painting. Ideally, a good composition directs the viewer's eye in and around the painting through the effective use of shape, color, and line. These elements create a visual path that leads to the intended center of interest, or *focal point*. In a strong composition, the focal point is typically placed off-center to create more interest. In addition, good compositions usually contain overlapping objects to provide a sense of depth. This painting of a scenic hillside dotted with houses in Ravello, Italy, follows the rules of good composition. The arch serves to direct and frame the viewer's gaze, leading the eye to focus on the sunlit buildings, which are staggered at different heights and overlap one another to add dimension. And a deliberately asymmetrical distribution of shadows, buildings, and foliage shifts attention away from the direct center of the composition, resulting in a more dynamic painting.

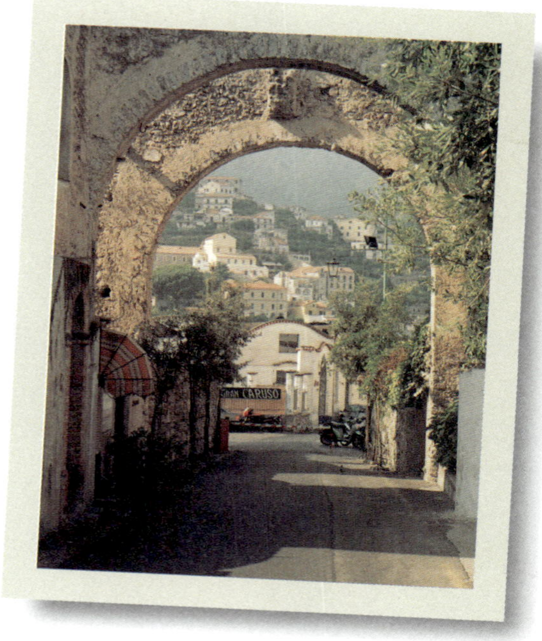

FRAMING THE COMPOSITION Because the arch frames the hillside, this composition starts strong. But every composition can be enhanced; here I crop the foreground of my reference to bring the point of view forward.

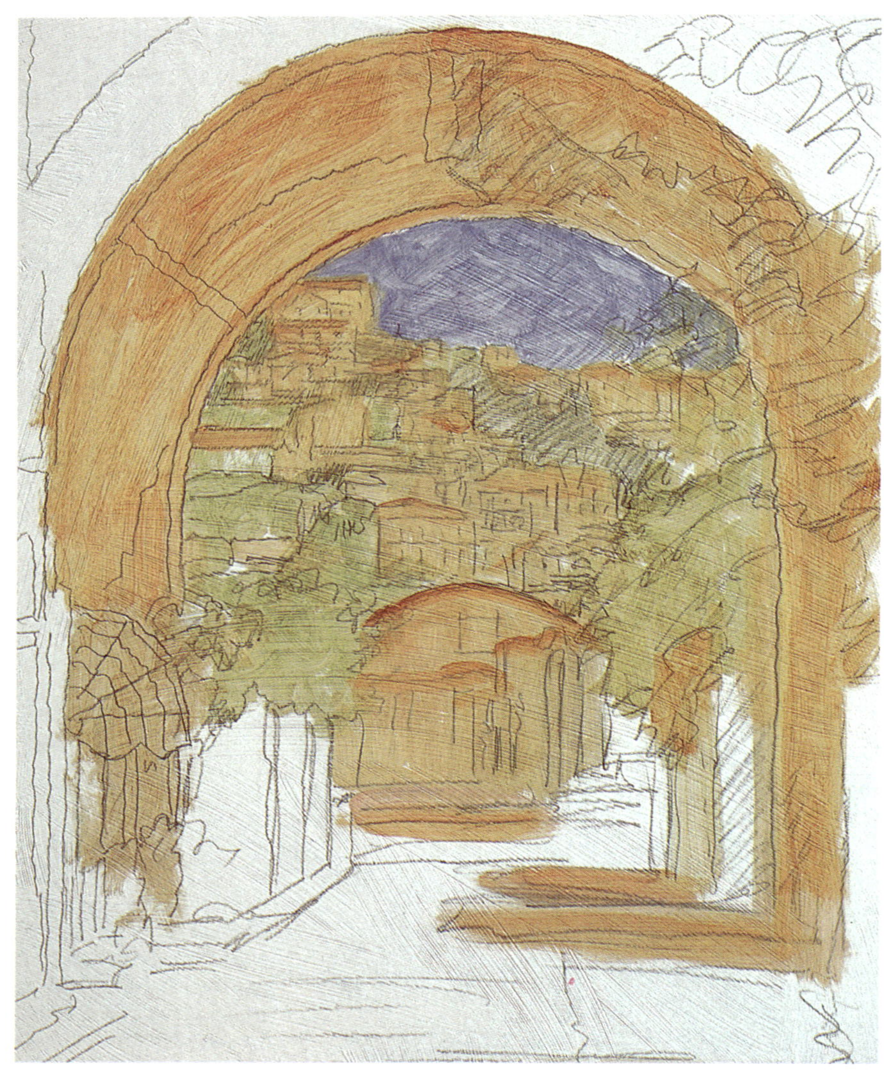

1 To create texture, I start layering gesso onto a masonite panel, applying thick, sweeping strokes with a large brush. When the gesso is dry, I sketch the scene and, using a water-color approach, begin layering transparent, water-thinned colors. First I add blue-violet to the sky with a medium round bristle brush. For the archway and buildings, I use variations of raw sienna mixed with Naples yellow and unbleached titanium. I block in the trees with sap green.

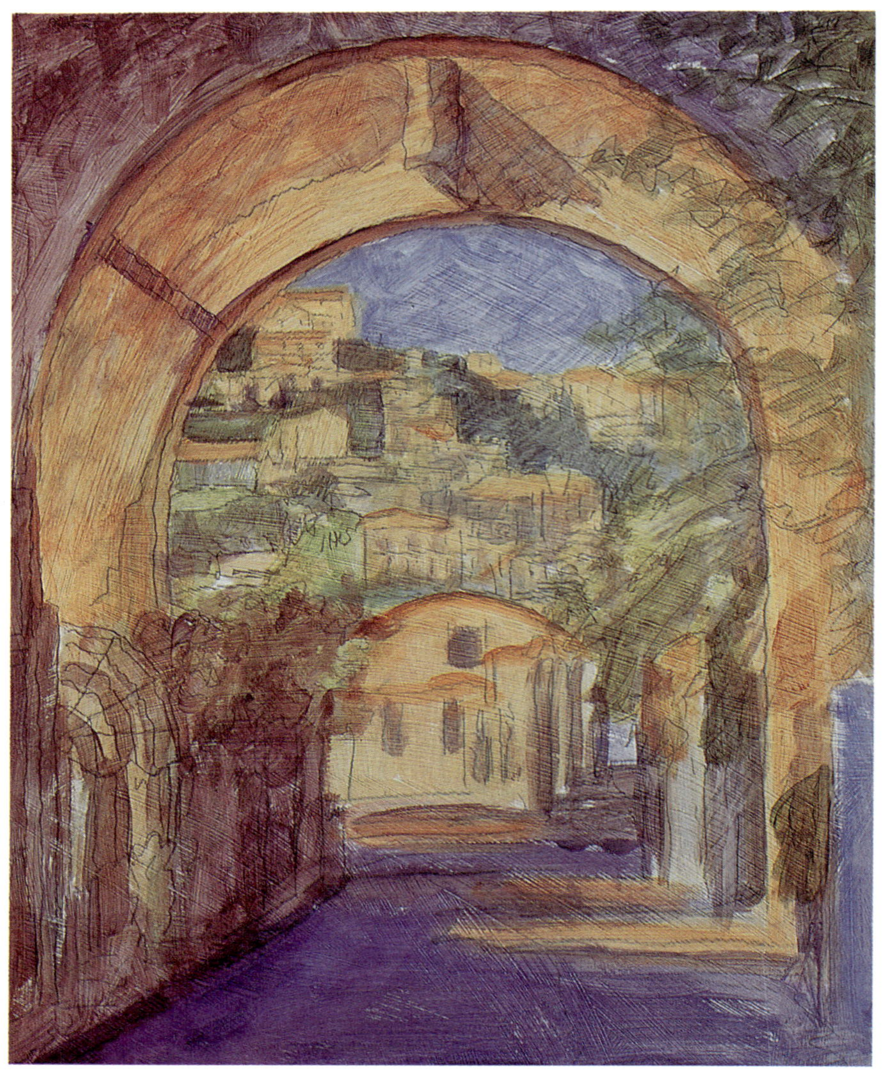

2 Working from light to dark, next I'll add the cooler areas of shadow. As in the first step, I thin the color with a little water before applying it to the masonite with a medium round bristle brush. I block in the foreground archway with burnt sienna mixed with dioxazine purple. Then, to paint the street, I use a mixture of dioxazine purple and light blue-violet. For the details around the edges, I use less water to create thicker paint mixtures.

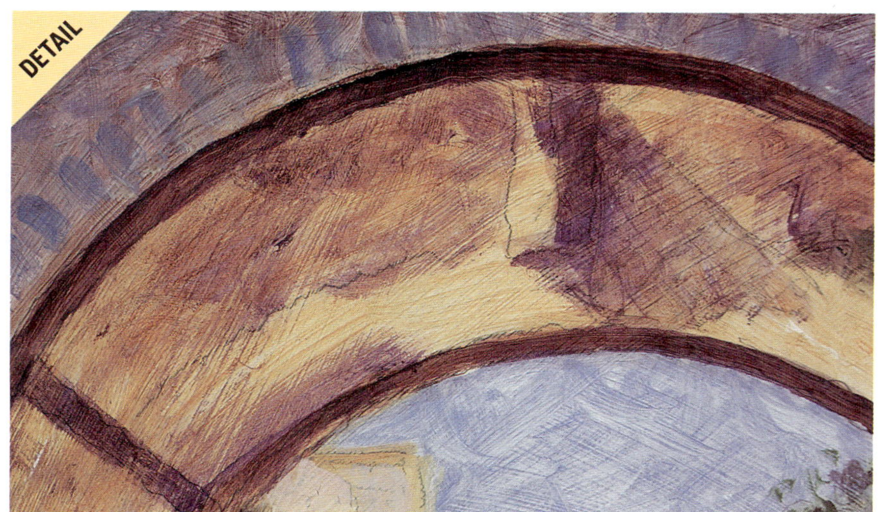

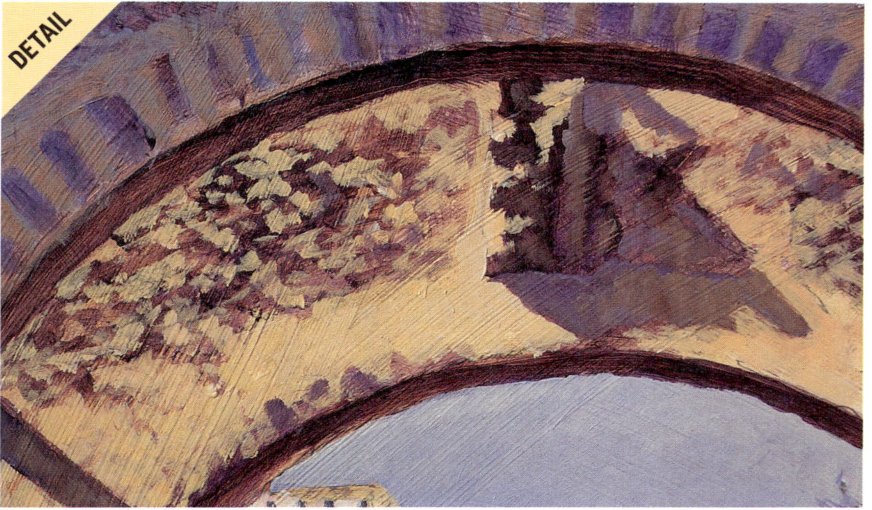

◄ **CREATING THE APPEARANCE OF AGE** Because this old-world arch has stood the test of time, it wouldn't do to paint it with even, smooth color. Instead I deliberately make sharp delineations between the dark and light values, applying the color with visible brushstrokes for a more weathered effect.

◄ **BUILDING TEXTURE** Now the stark contrasts in color take on the appearance of worn paint. The lighter tones attract the eye and seem to "pop" forward, while the darker purples and grays appear to recede, creating a mottled appearance with more than one level. Notice that I used the dark purples and grays to "draw" a few cracks and chips in the architecture, contributing to the worn look of the arch.

GRAYED UNDERPAINTING COLORS

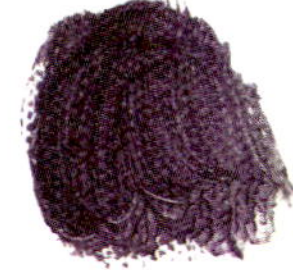

Dioxazine purple + burnt sienna

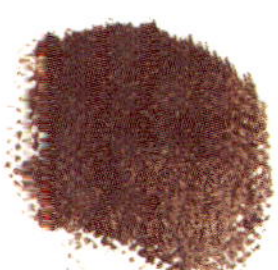

Burnt sienna + Payne's gray

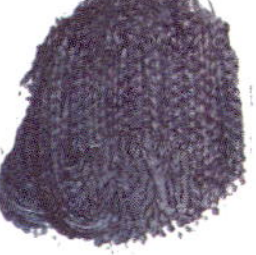

Cerulean blue + Payne's gray

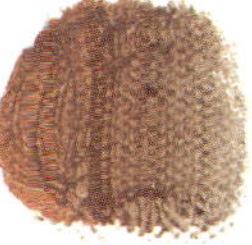

Raw sienna + Payne's gray

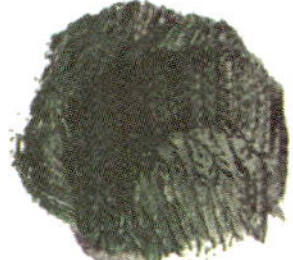

Sap green + Payne's gray

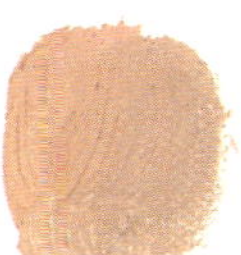

Light portrait pink + Payne's gray

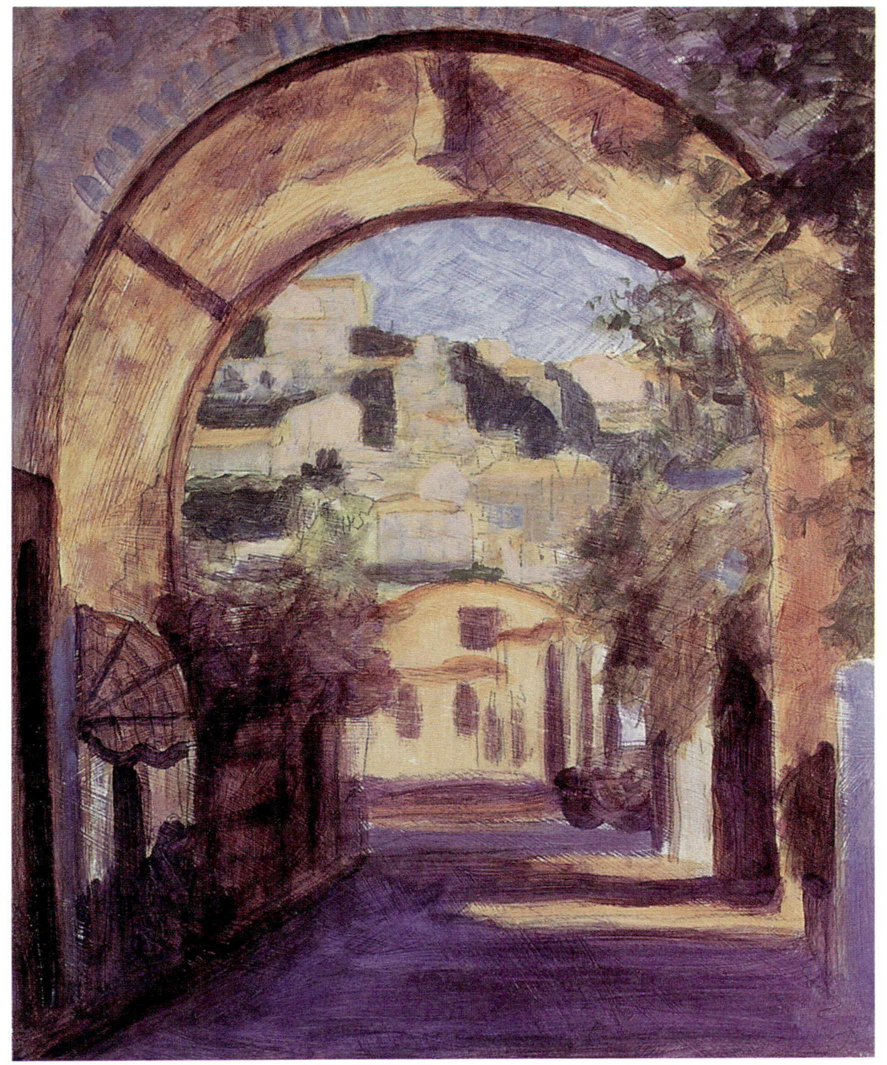

3 Now I strengthen the darkest values of the scene. I switch to a medium flat sable brush so that I can paint with a little more detail, but I still keep my brushstrokes relatively loose and suggestive. Using light blue-violet, yellow oxide, and a few slightly grayed colors (see color samples above right), I continue blocking in the largest areas of color, which will serve as an underpainting for the highlights to follow.

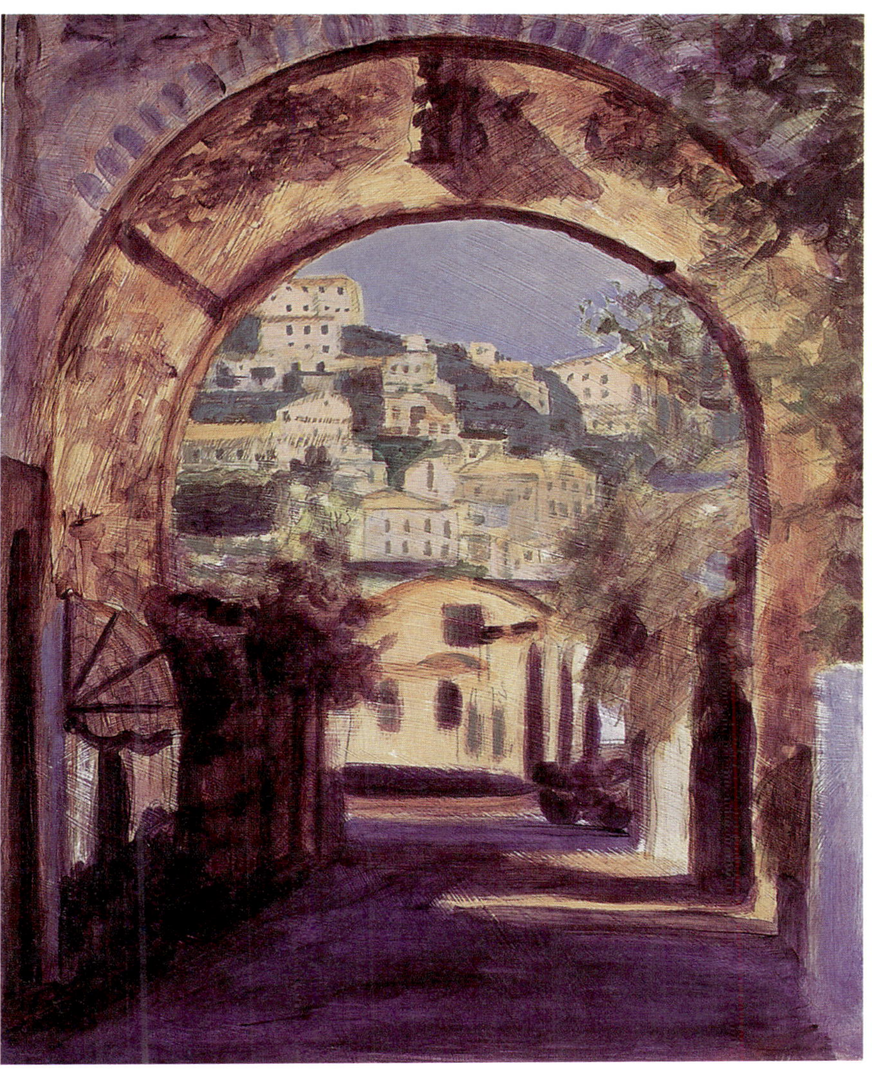

4 In the background, I paint the trees with mixes of the various greens and blues already on my palette and suggest windows and architectural details with Payne's gray. I layer a more opaque mix of light blue-violet and light portrait pink over the sky. Then I darken the foreground shadows: In the archway, I use dioxazine purple mixed with burnt sienna; on the street, I switch to dioxazine purple mixed with Payne's gray and cerulean blue.

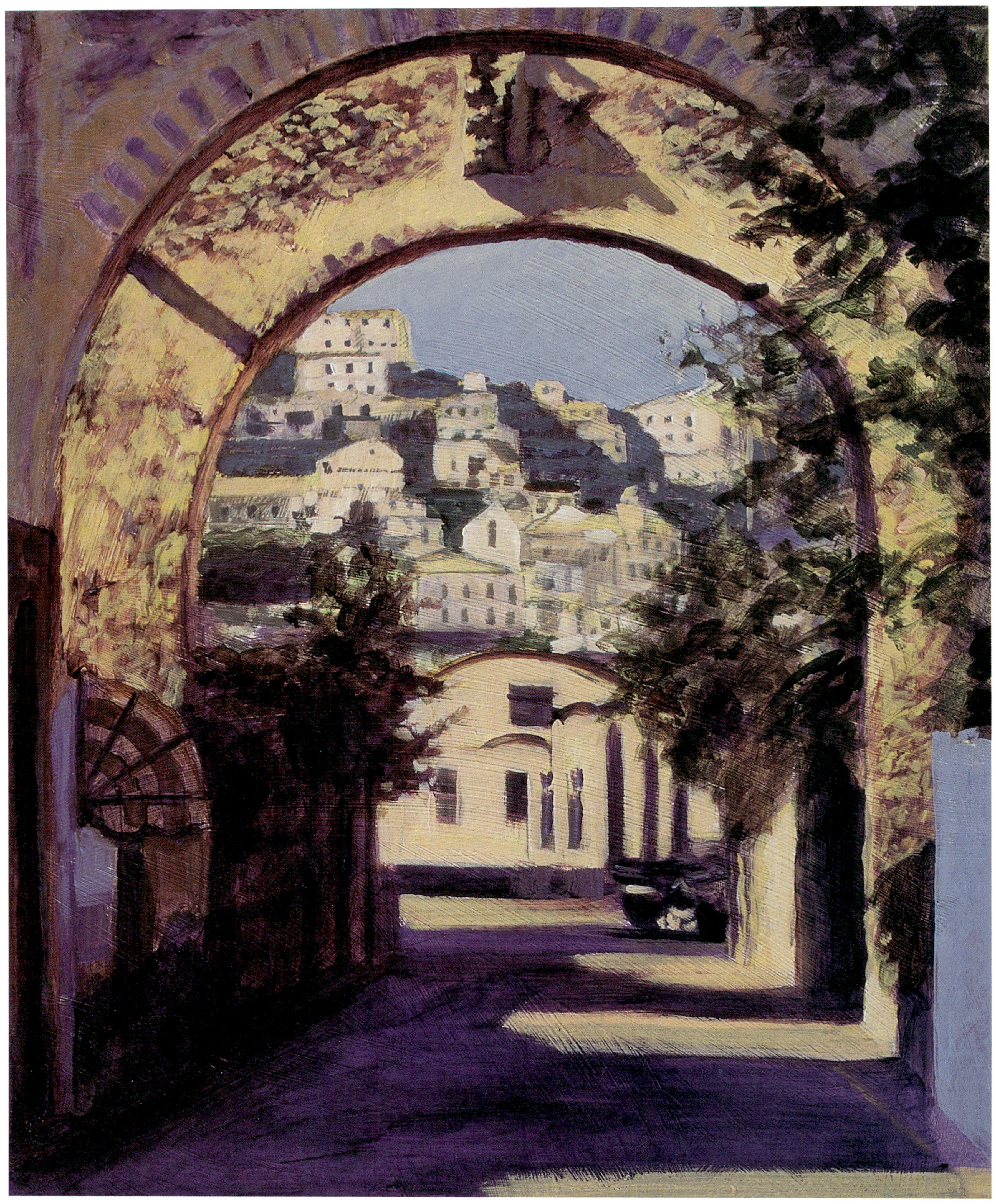

5 Up to this stage, I've been working from light to dark; but now it's time to bring up the highlights. First I mix a few variations of Naples yellow, chrome orange, light portrait pink, and unbleached titanium. Then I add gloss medium to the mix before drybrushing it onto the sunlit parts of the archway and buildings with a medium flat sable brush. Next I add a layer of color to the foreground using burnt sienna mixed with light blue-violet and raw sienna. I use the same colors to lighten the shadows a touch and to add more detail to the inner arch. Then I brighten the sky with light blue-violet mixed with titanium white, a touch of cadmium yellow medium, and glazing medium. I also apply sap green mixed with Payne's gray to the foliage for contrast, and I add a few more foreground details with a mix of light blue-violet, raw sienna, and dioxazine purple.

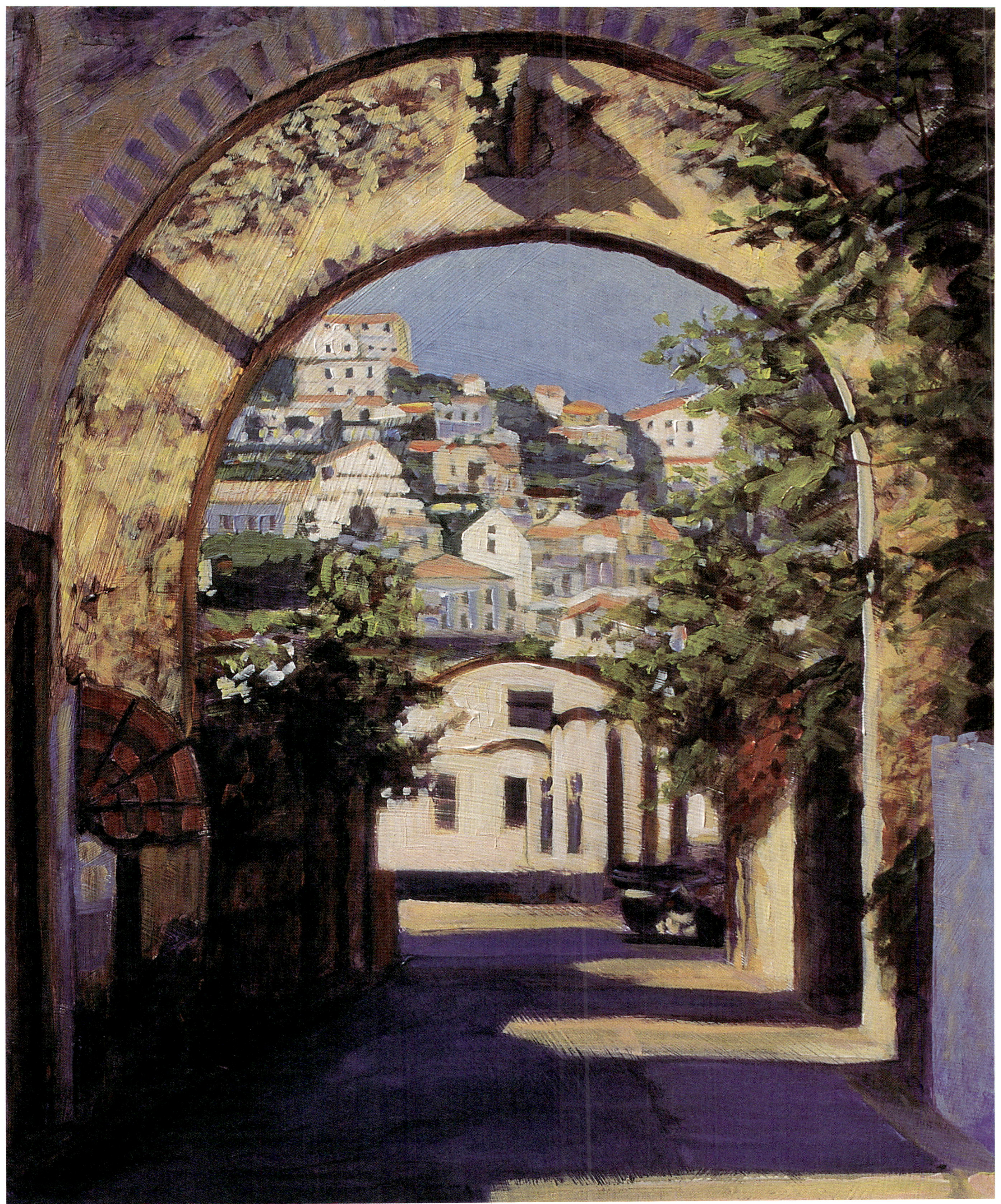

6 Now my darks and lights are firmly established, but the painting isn't quite complete. I still need to add dashes of color to bring everything together. With a warm mix of magenta, chrome orange, and titanium white, I dab the suggestion of rooftops on the hillside in the background, switching to a mix of light blue-violet, dioxazine purple, and titanium white to give the impression of distant buildings. Then I brighten the foliage a little, applying sap green mixed with chromium oxide green, cadmium yellow medium, and chrome orange. For interest and texture, I vary the thickness of the paint. At this stage, I also apply cadmium red light mixed with Payne's gray to the canopy on the left side of the archway. The warm colors of the composition attract the eye and help direct the viewer's gaze, first from the red canopy in the foreground to the warm foliage in the middle ground, and then back toward the focal point.

Using Atmospheric Perspective

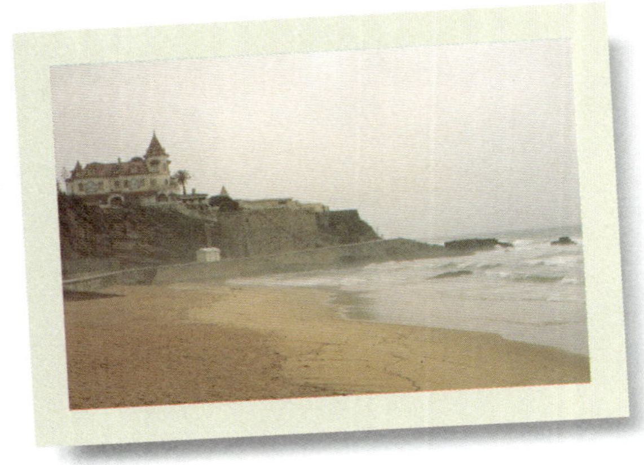

PAINTING MISTY WEATHER As you can see from my reference, the misty atmosphere dulls distant elements as usual; but, to a somewhat lesser degree, it also mutes the color and softens the detail of closer elements.

When painting outdoor scenes, employing atmospheric perspective is critical. Outside, impurities in the air (such as moisture and dust) block out some sunlight, so objects in the distance appear less distinct and with softer edges than do objects in the foreground. And because the longer, red wavelengths of light are filtered out, things in the distance also appear cooler and bluer. I capture the hazy atmosphere of this coastal scene in Cascais, Portugal, by applying the rules of atmospheric perspective—painting the elements in the distance and objects farther away with less detail and with bluer, more muted colors, while saving the brightest colors and the most detail for the foreground.

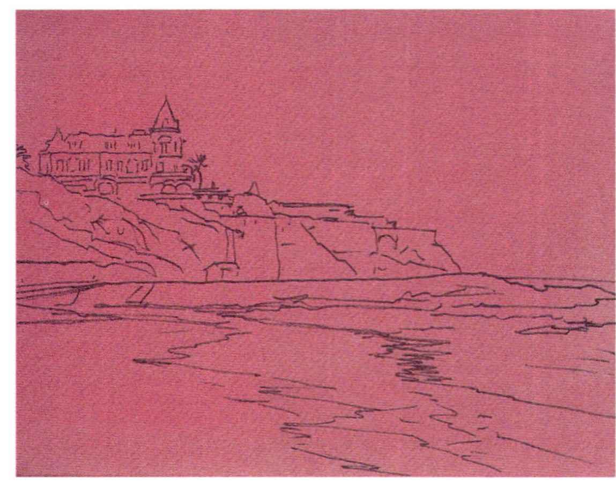

1 I begin with a simple sketch, using a fine-point black marker on a medium-textured, stretched canvas. Over the sketch, I apply a thin wash of magenta, covering the entire canvas. The magenta underpainting will add warmth to the final painting, preventing it from appearing too gloomy.

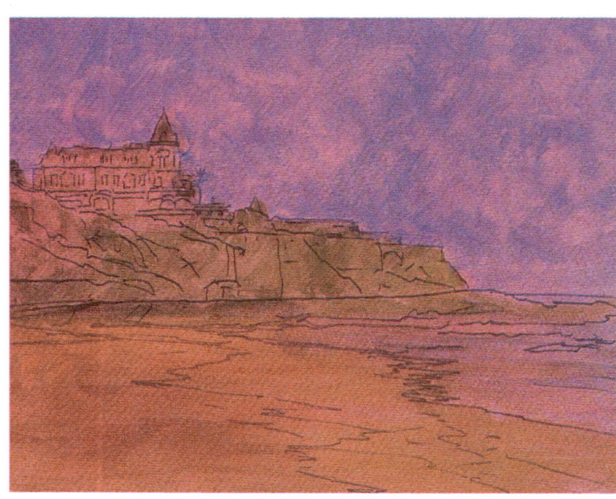

2 Using cerulean blue, sap green, red oxide, and yellow oxide, I start blocking in the color. Beginning with the sky and working down, I mix the paints with gloss medium and a little water. I dull the colors with a little Payne's gray before applying them thinly with a large, flat bristle brush.

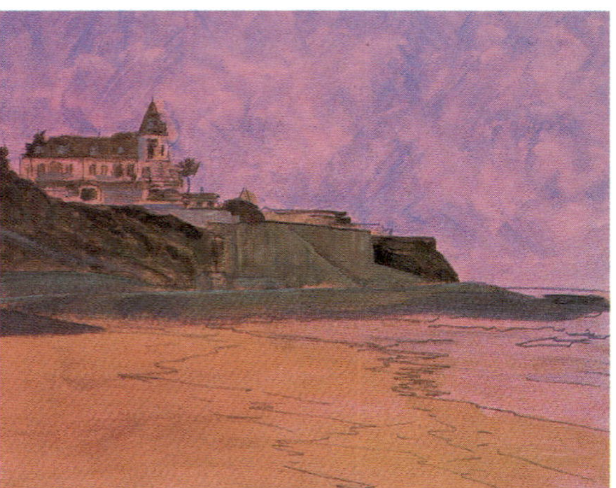

3 Next I add dark tones to the building, cliffs, and seawall with various mixes of burnt sienna with dioxazine purple. I use a little unbleached titanium to lighten the values and gel medium to thicken the paint. A slightly smaller flat sable brush allows me to "draw" with a bit more detail.

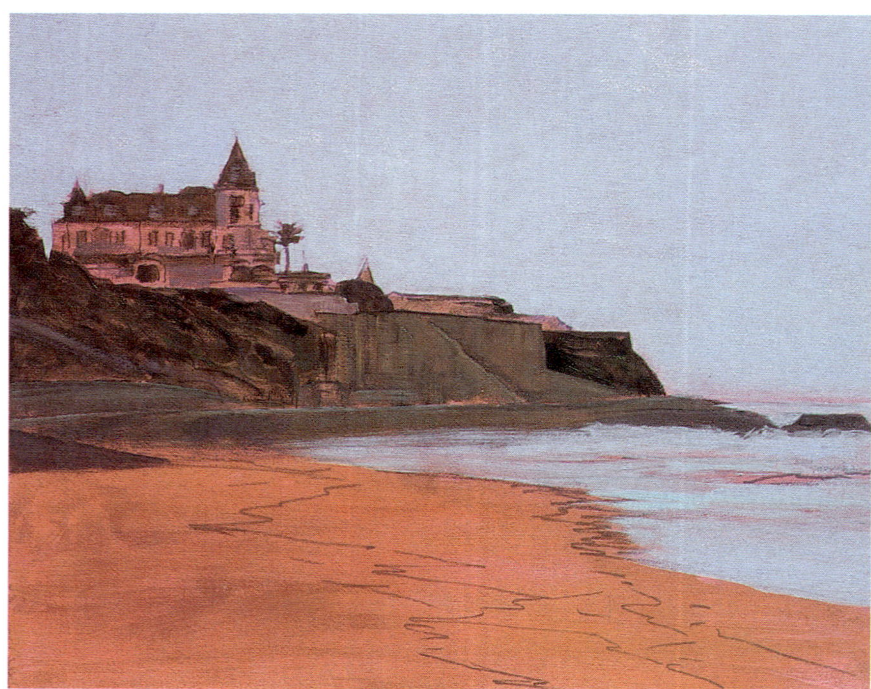

4 Next I develop the sky and water, using the same technique for both. For more opacity, I add gel medium to a mix of cerulean blue, light blue-violet, Payne's gray, and white, but I allow enough transparency for some of the underpainting to show through. In the water, I leave gaps where the surf will be rendered. Notice I pull some of the paint up into the rocks to establish waves, softening the edges of the water where it meets the beach with drybrush.

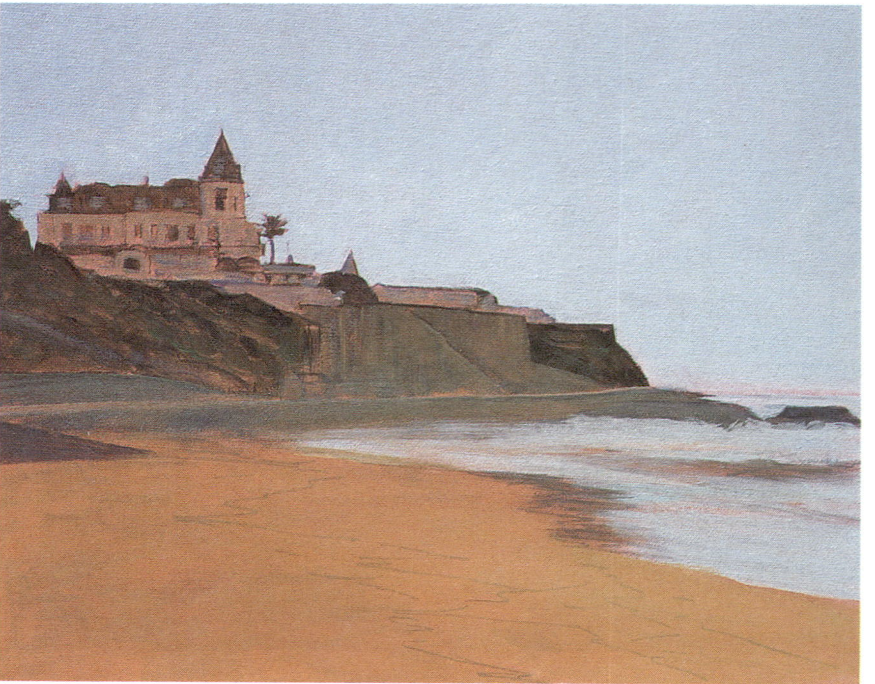

5 To soften the dark tones, I add another layer of color using various mixtures of red oxide, yellow oxide, and Payne's gray. I paint the lighter colors of the building and the wall with mixtures of light blue-violet, Payne's gray, and unbleached titanium, using the edge of a small, flat brush to define the shapes. Finally I apply a lighter value of transparent yellow oxide to the beach.

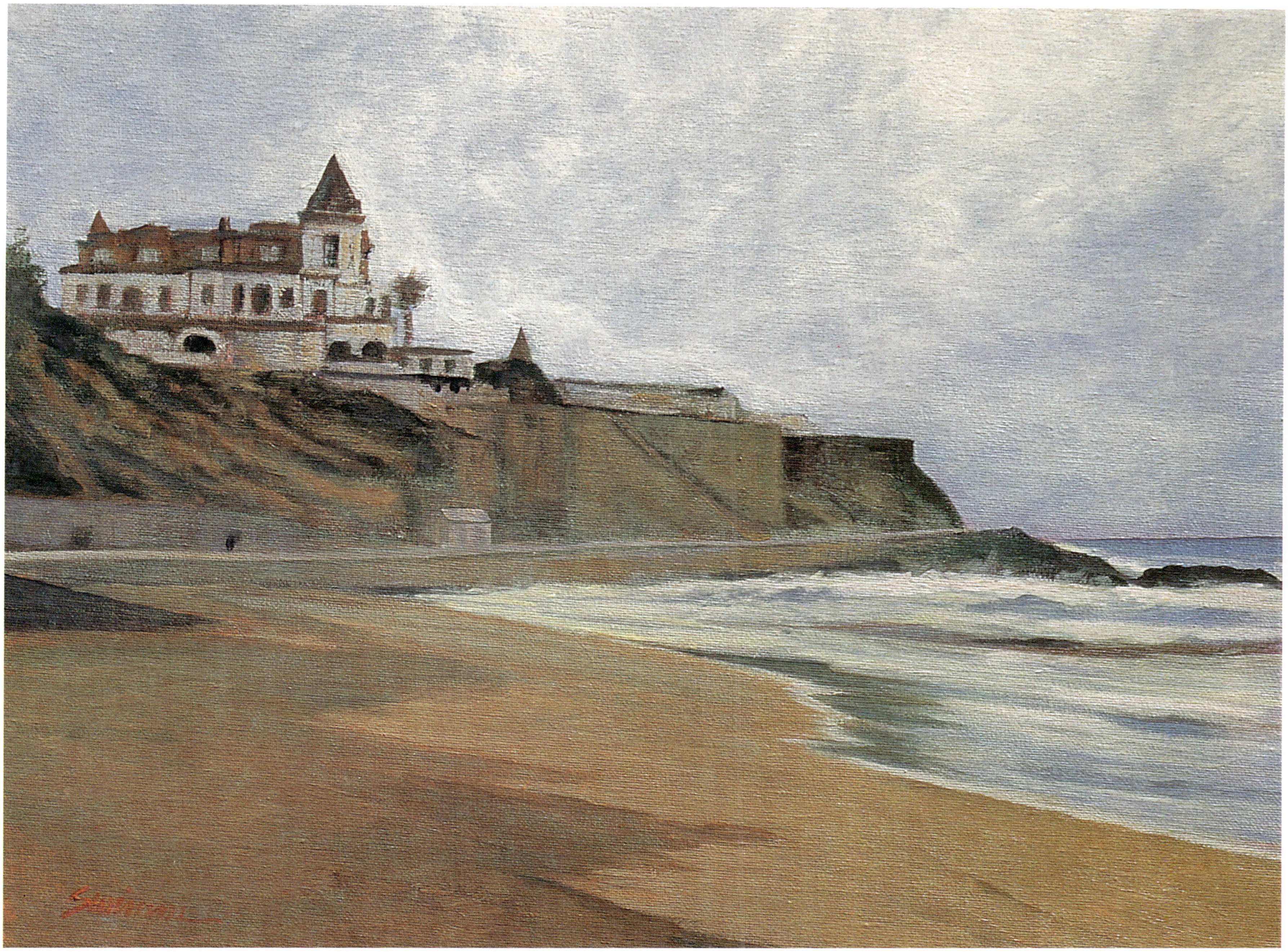

8 Adding a little unbleached titanium and Payne's gray to the colors already on my palette gives me the colors I need for final details and adjustments. With these mixes, I continue to refine details on the cliffs and the building. I also add another layer of color to the beach, this one more opaque. I keep the mix closest to the beach light, adding more Payne's gray, sap green, and burnt sienna for the dark areas on the left of the composition. To finish, I darken the horizon line and the details in the water and along the edge of the sand.

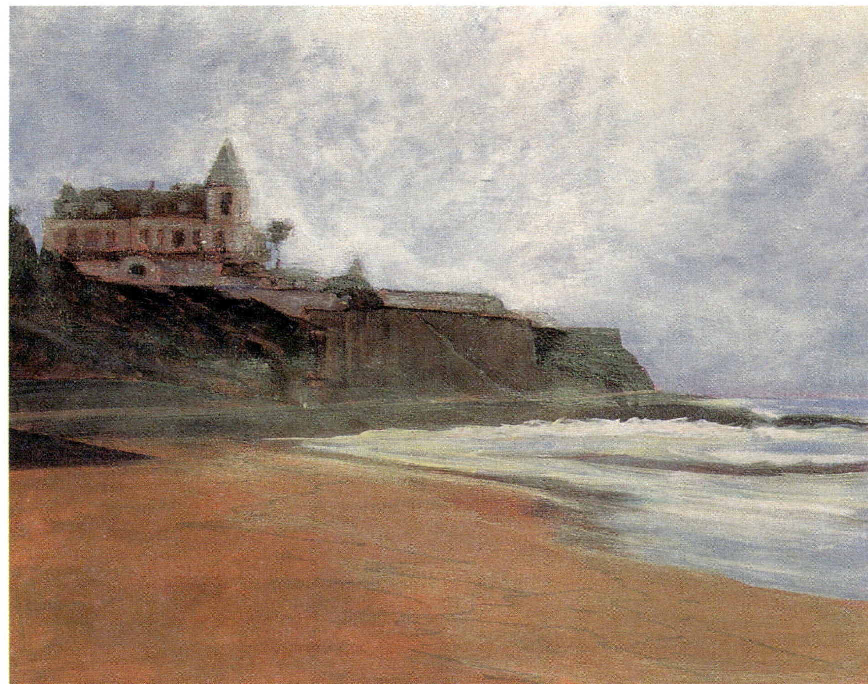

6 Now I add yet another layer of color—this time a thin glaze that covers the entire canvas. Mixing light blue-violet with light portrait pink, unbleached titanium, and a generous amount of acrylic glazing medium, I apply transparent color using large brushstrokes. I apply a thicker glaze over the sky and water to create a sense of clouds and surf, working the paint into the surface. (You can pull off the glaze with a dry brush if it gets too thick.)

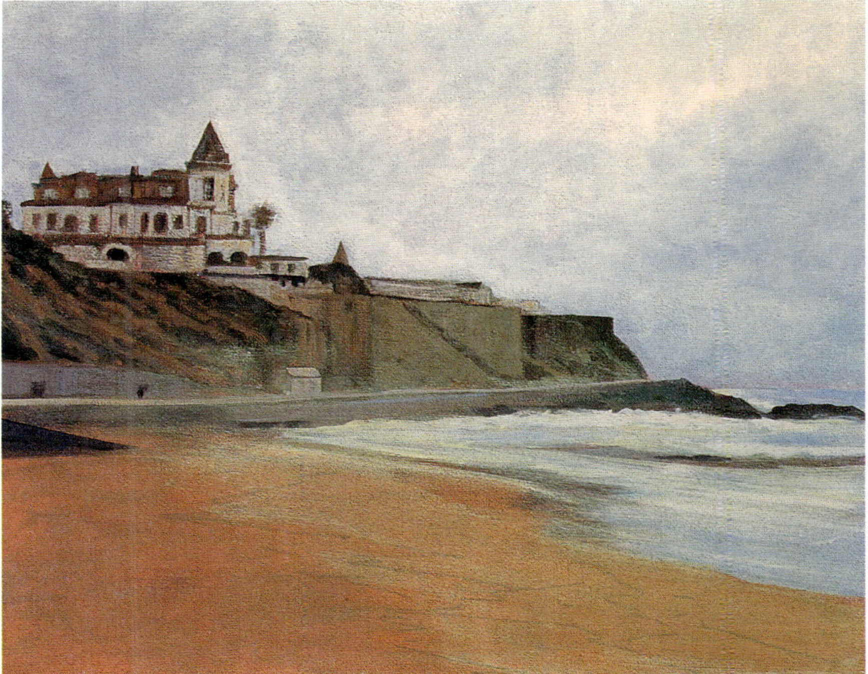

7 Starting with a muted, bluish-gray mixture of dioxazine purple, Payne's gray, and titanium white, I add building details with the the edge of a medium flat sable brush. For variation, I also use light blue-violet mixed with Payne's gray and sap green mixed with light blue-violet and Payne's gray. For the windows, rooftops, cliffs, and seawall, I apply brownish mixtures of unbleached titanium with Payne's gray and either alizarin crimson or burnt sienna.

EXPLORING LIGHT AND SHADOW

The interplay between light and shadow can pique a viewer's interest in a scene. Incorporating subtle, natural contrasts between light and dark—such as those evident in the early morning or late afternoon—can also add vitality to a painting. At those times of day (when the sun is lower in the sky), long, cool shadows provide contrast to warm sunlit patches. In this painting of a quaint street in Lucca, Italy, I create the illusion of dappled sunlight through the use of color and value. A range of cool values and spots of reflected light in the shadows pair with intense color to make this street scene compelling and inviting.

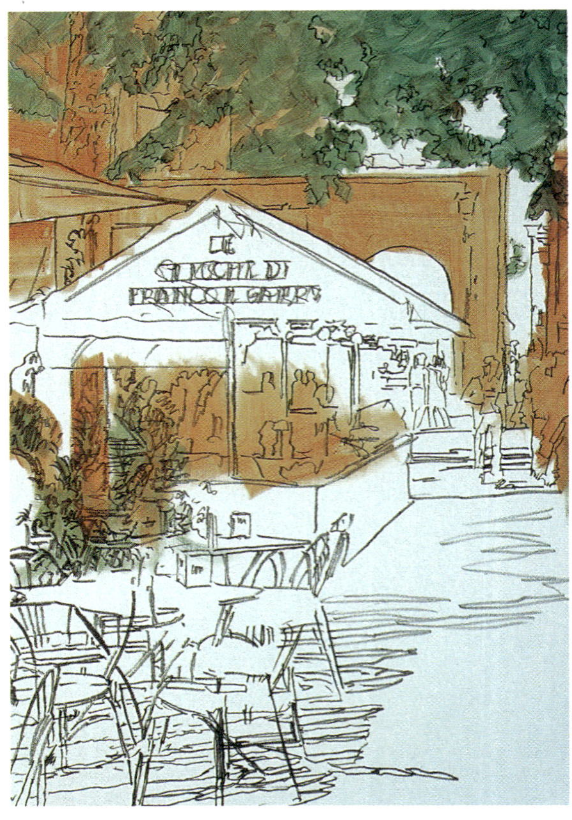

1 After sketching, I use a large flat sable brush to wash over the buildings with a mix of raw sienna, sap green, and gloss medium, adding burnt sienna for the dark areas. For foliage, I use phthalo green mixed with Payne's gray.

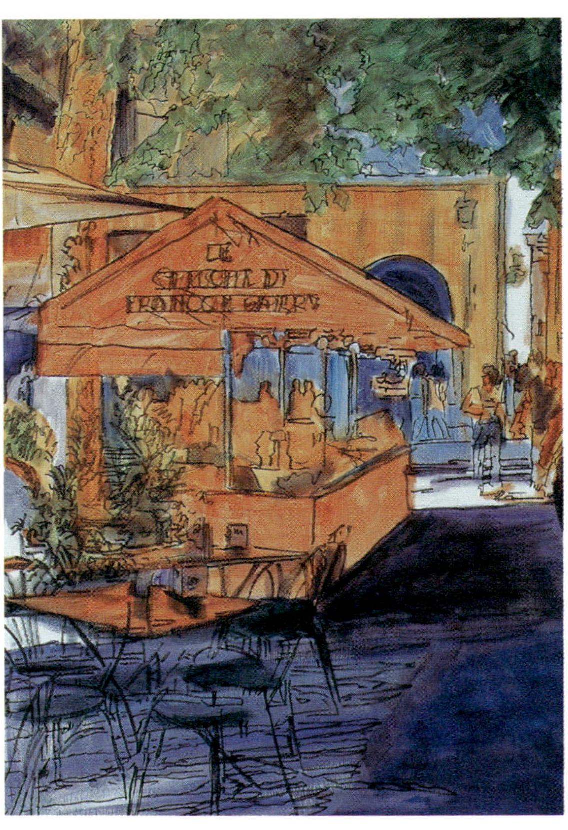

2 I block in the cart and tables with burnt sienna, using a mix of dioxazine purple, Payne's gray, and cerulean blue in the shadows. For the distant shadows, wall, and figures, I mix dioxazine purple, phthalo blue, and light blue-violet.

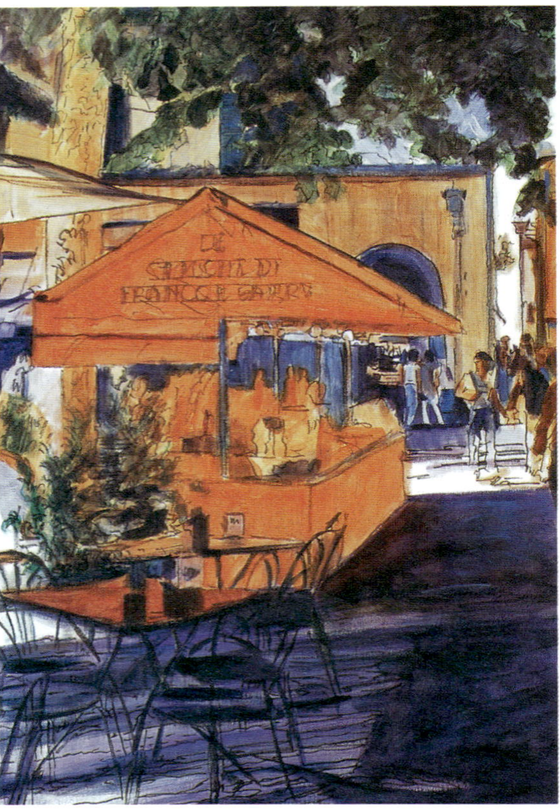

3 Now I lay in dark colors that will serve as an underpainting for the highlights. I apply darks to the foliage, along with background and foreground shadows. And I also glaze over the cart and tables. (See color samples on page 11.)

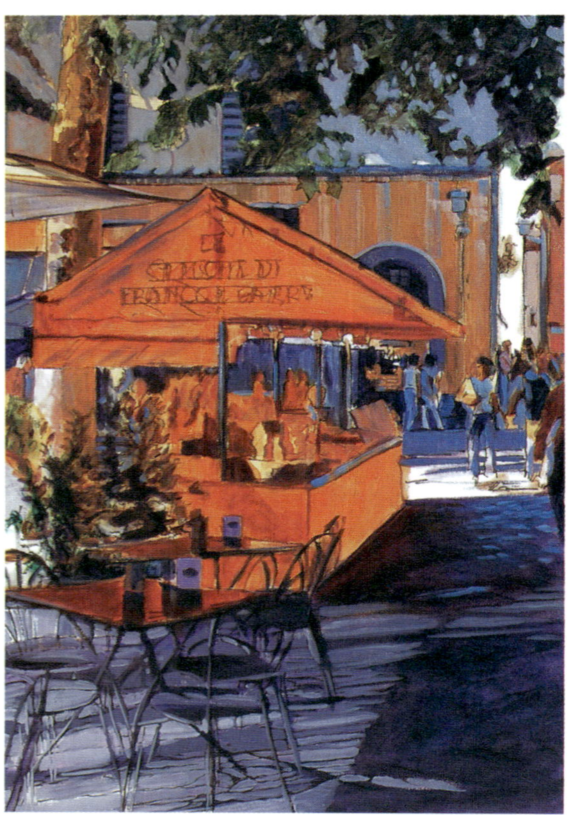

4 Next I mix a few purples. (See color samples on page 11.) I apply these more opaque colors to the foreground shadows with a medium flat sable brush. For harmony, I also work these colors into shadows throughout the scene. Next I apply color to the tree trunk using variations of burnt sienna mixed with magenta, raw sienna, dioxazine purple, and light blue-violet. Then I add light blue-violet, white, and bronze yellow to the purple mixes for the area where the building peeks through the foliage. On the building, I drybrush a mix of magenta, raw sienna, and light blue-violet, using dioxazine purple mixed with cerulean blue in the arch.

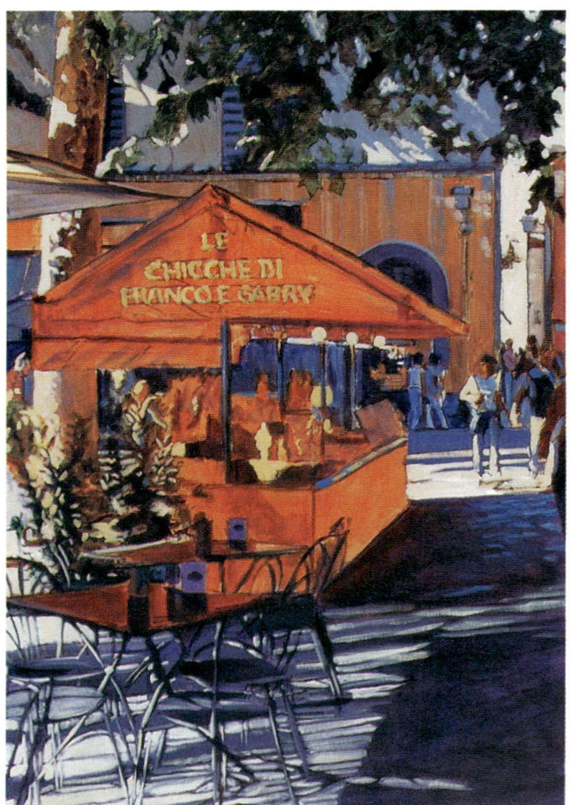

5 It's now time for the first layer of highlights. I begin by mixing light portrait pink with yellow oxide for the lettering on the canopy, which I quickly and loosely apply with the edge of the medium flat brush. For the more opaque highlights in the trees and building, I add unbleached titanium to the lettering mix. Then, with light portrait pink mixed with yellow oxide and a little blue-violet, I use drybrush to add highlights to the street and foreground.

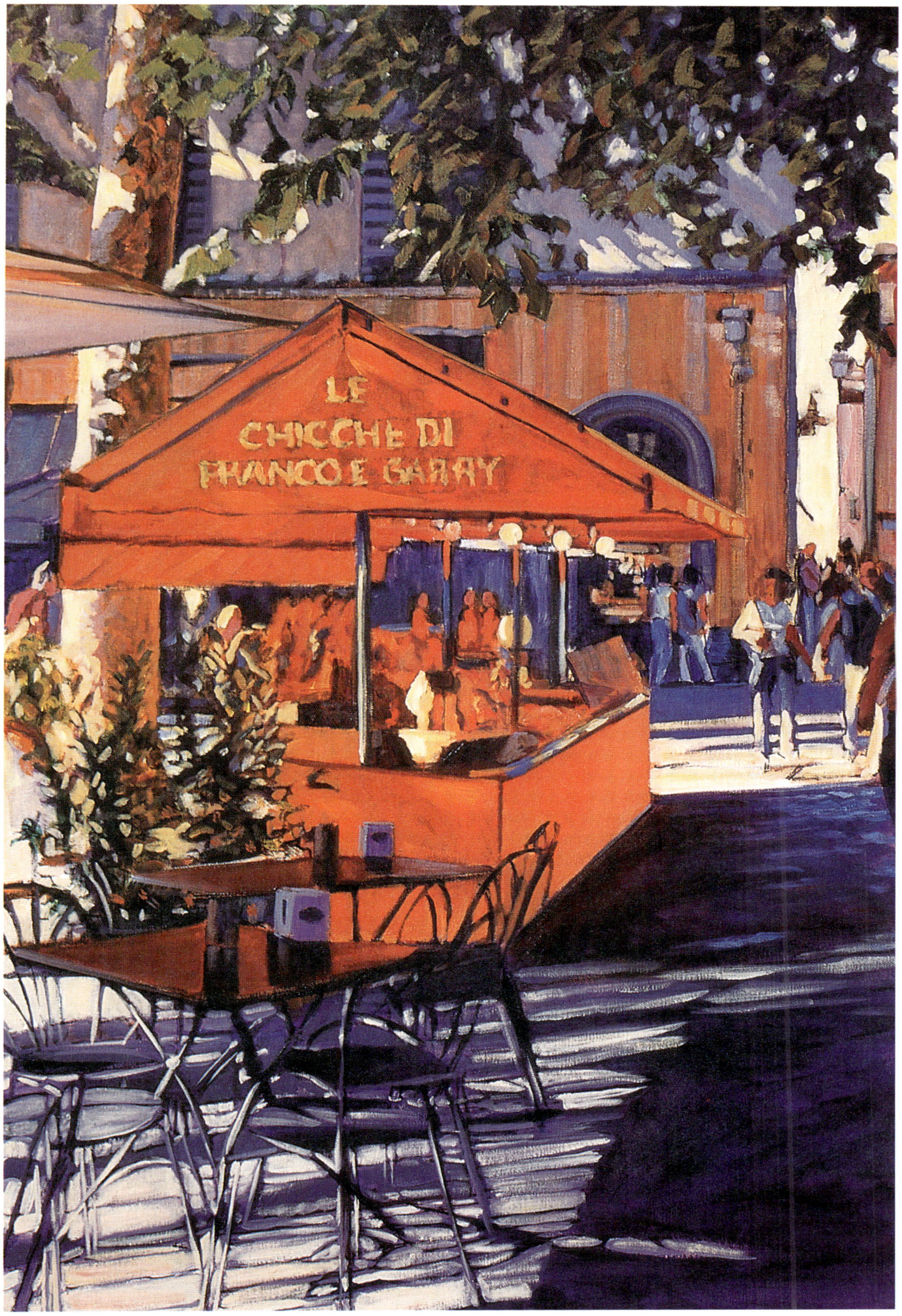

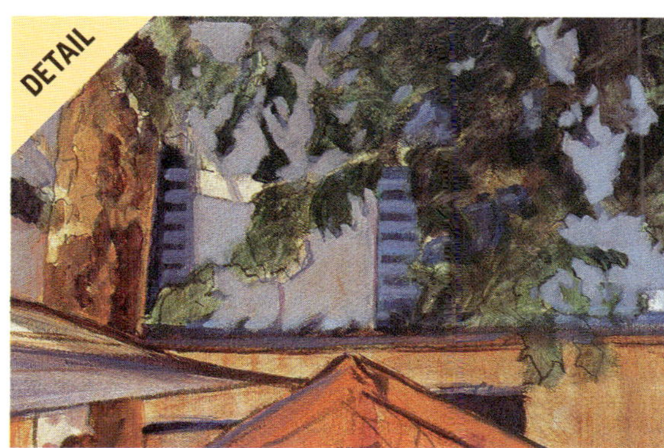

CREATING DIMENSION To make the foliage appear to come forward in the scene, rather than lying flat against the façade, I employ light and shadow. By applying light values to highlight the foliage itself, the leaves appear to come forward in the painting, especially in contrast to the shadowed building.

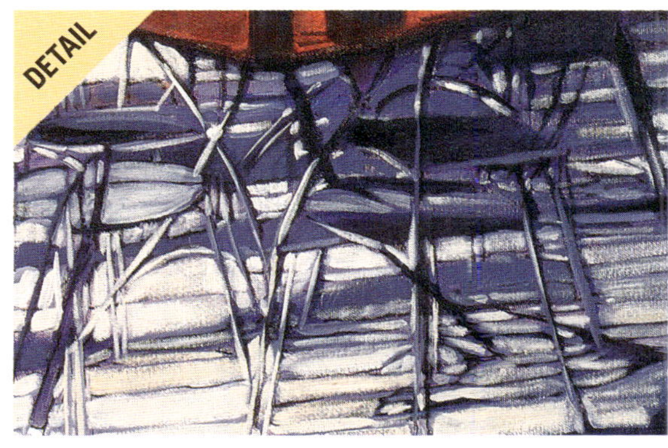

"DRAWING" HIGHLIGHTS To give dimension to the thin chairs and table, I use my brush as a drawing tool. (See page 3.) I separate light and shadow areas by applying highlights with a more opaque layer of paint, using the edge of a flat sable brush. Although using the brush's edge gives me more control, I don't worry too much about precision—shadows and highlights are naturally asymmetrical, so perfectly straight lines would appear out of place.

6 A few final light color applications will finish the painting. I add color to the foliage with mixtures of sap green, raw oxide, bronze yellow, and red-orange, applying the color randomly and varying the brushstrokes. For contrast, I make sure to retain some of the shadow areas. I also add a more opaque layer of color to the canopy, this time using a brighter mixture of burnt sienna and red-orange; and, for additional highlights, I add spots of cadmium orange mixed with cadmium yellow light.

COOL FOREGROUND SHADOW VARIATIONS

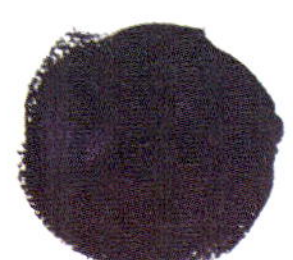

Dioxazine purple + Payne's gray + titanium white

Dioxazine purple + more Payne's gray + more titanium white

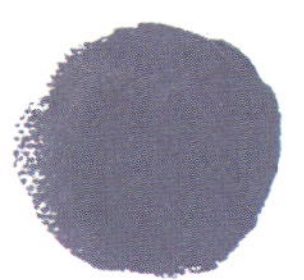

More dioxazine purple + Payne's gray + more titanium white

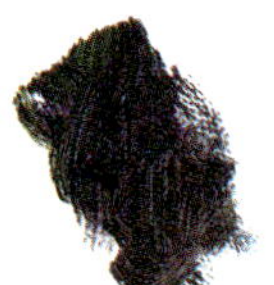

FOLIAGE DARKS
Phthalo green + dioxazine purple + Payne's gray

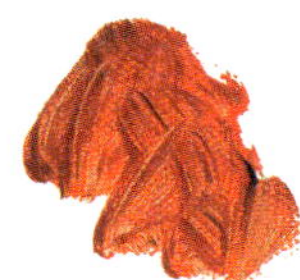

CART AND TABLETOP GLAZE
Burnt sienna + red-orange + glazing medium

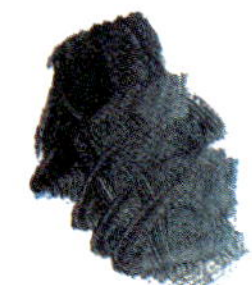

FOREGROUND SHADOWS
Phthalo blue + light blue-violet + Payne's gray

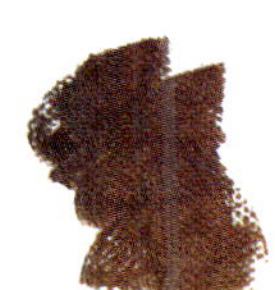

BACKGROUND SHADOWS
Burnt sienna + dioxazine purple

FOLLOWING A PHOTO REFERENCE

Capturing fleeting images presents artists with a timing challenge. One way to meet this challenge is by using photo references. A photo stops the action, providing you the luxury of time and allowing you the chance to study a scene before you begin painting. This double waterfall (called "Wailua Falls") on the island of Kauai, Hawaii, is captivating because of its dimension and movement. So, to paint a subject whose beauty relies on its constant state of flux, I first captured the free-flowing waters on film.

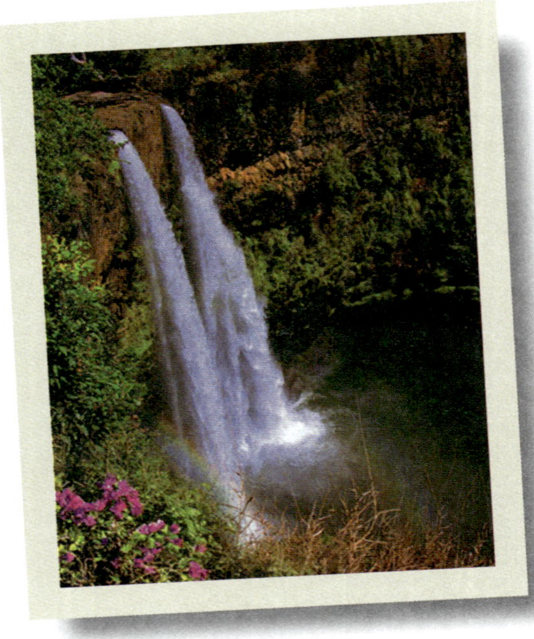

STUDYING THE SCENE **Although I enjoy painting outdoors, painting this scene *en plein air* may have caused me to overlook some of the more nuanced elements of this scene—such as the faint rainbow at the base of the waterfall. With my photo in hand, I can take the time to carefully study the scene and all its detail.**

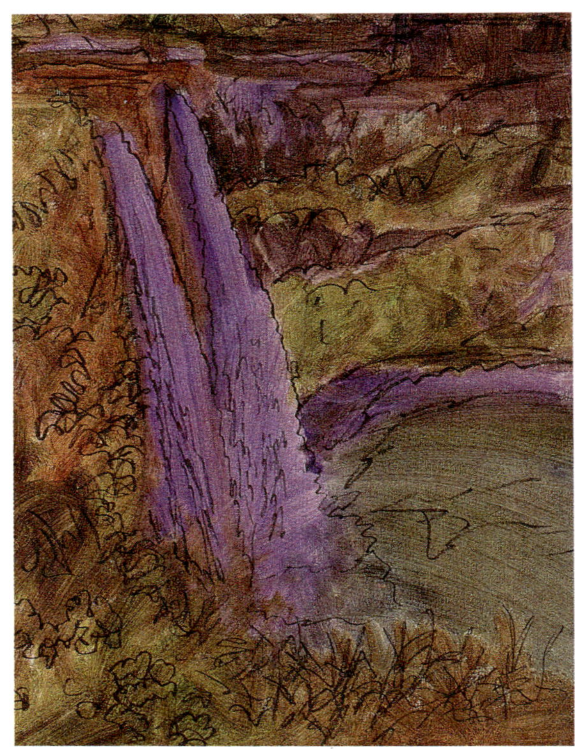

1 **I quickly sketch the scene, focusing on the key elements. Then, using a large flat bristle brush, I begin blocking in color. To improve the flow of the paints, I mix in some gloss medium. I also add some water to keep this layer relatively transparent. I start applying dioxazine purple to the waterfall and some shadow areas; variations of sap green mixed with burnt sienna to the cliffs and foliage; and sap green mixed with ultramarine blue to the pool of water below the falls.**

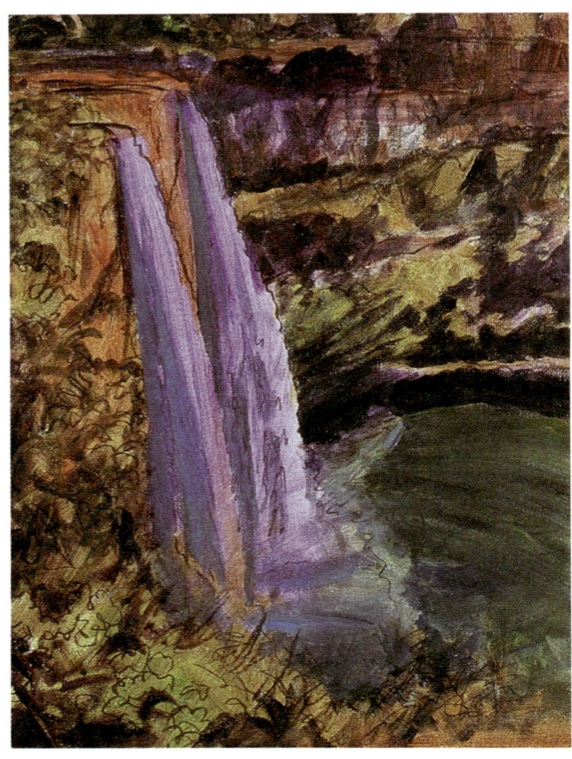

2 **Using a mix of sap green, Payne's gray, and light blue-violet, I block in the shadows of the waterfall, pulling down some of the color into the pool. To deepen the pool values, I mix sap green with ultramarine blue, applying the paint more thickly and using swirling brushstrokes to simulate the motion of the water. I also darken the cliffs and foliage, applying Payne's gray mixed with dioxazine purple and ultramarine blue.**

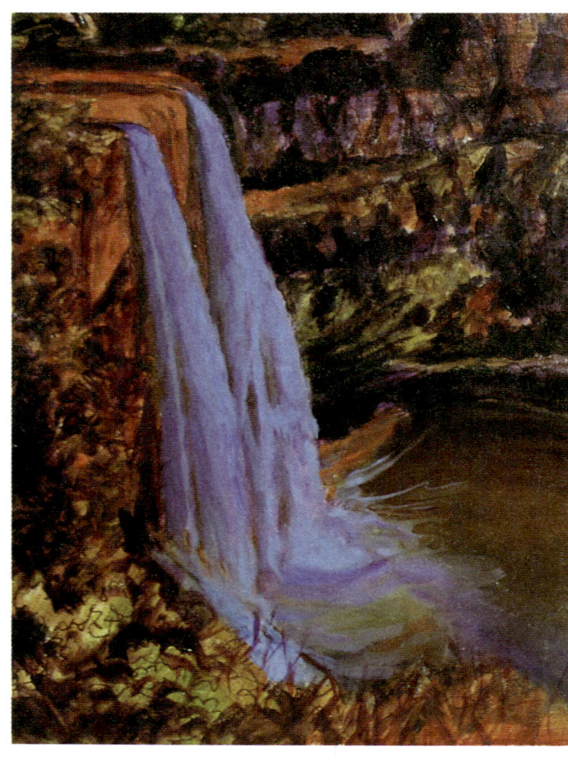

3 **Next I apply a mix of dioxazine purple, Payne's gray, and light blue-violet to the waterfall, blending a mix of ultramarine blue, sap green, and dioxazine purple into the pool. I also apply light blue-violet highlights. Then I apply more burnt sienna to the cliffs. And I also add dark values to the foliage using sap green mixed with Payne's gray, switching to Payne's gray mixed with burnt sienna for the cliffs.**

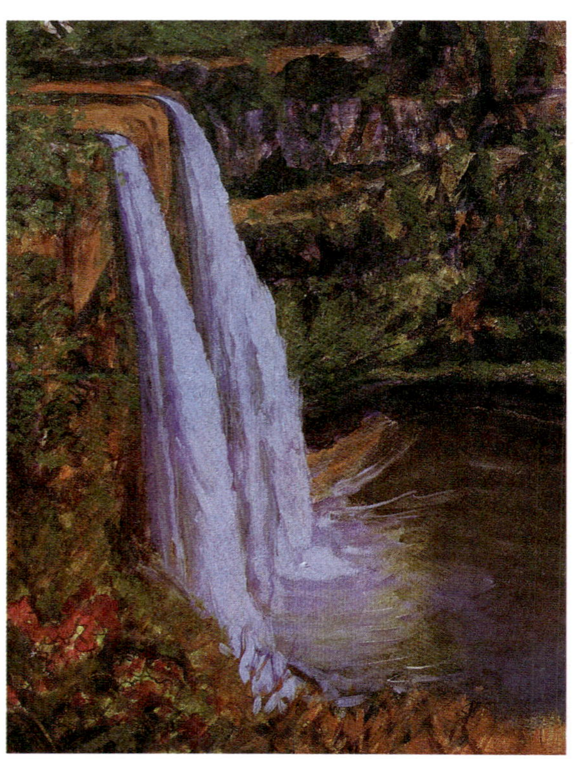

4 **To develop foliage detail, I mix emerald green with burnt sienna. Then I apply raw sienna to the cliffs and magenta to the foreground flowers. With a mix of dioxazine purple, light blue-violet, and Payne's gray, I apply highlights to the waterfall, "feathering" the edges with drybrush. Then I glaze over the pool, separately applying ultramarine blue, sap green, and raw sienna; then I blend the colors.**

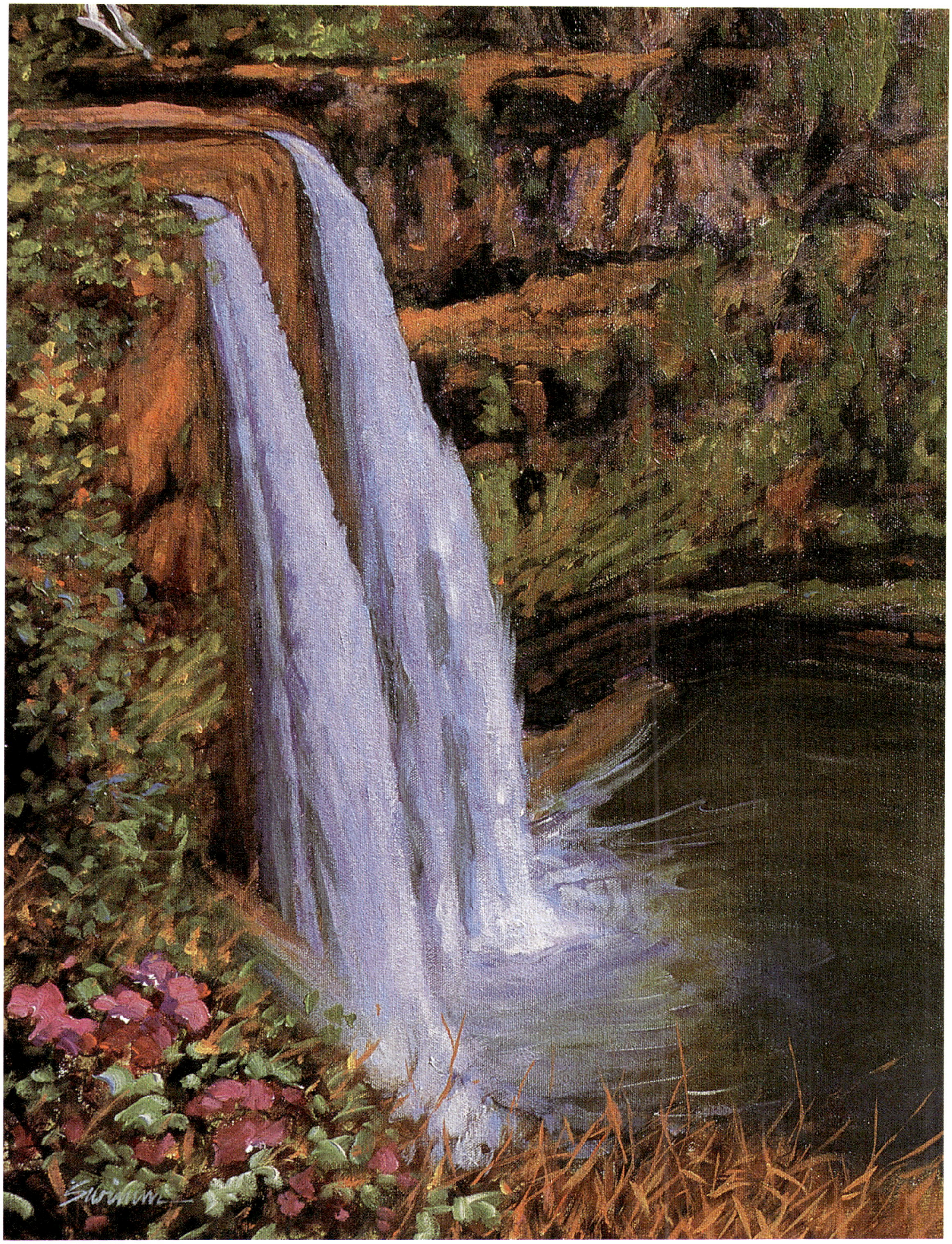

5 I finish the painting with brighter mixtures of paint, accentuating the highlights and refining the details. First I add final highlights to the waterfall using light blue-violet mixed with dioxazine purple and unbleached titanium. Next I drybrush color into the cliffs, using mixtures of red oxide, burnt sienna, and raw sienna, adding a little unbleached titanium for variation in the intensity. For the foliage, I use mixtures of sap green, bronze yellow, and cerulean blue, again adding unbleached titanium for lighter variations. I paint the flowers (see detail below) and then, for the finishing touches in the foreground, I use the edge of my brush to apply Naples yellow mixed with raw sienna and red oxide.

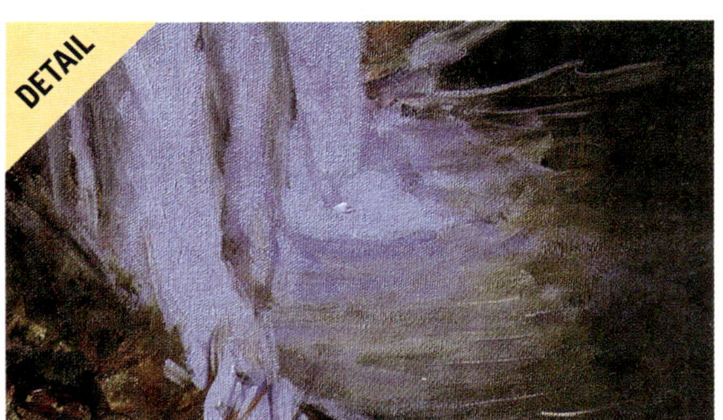

◄ DISTINGUISHING THE PAINTING FROM THE PHOTO
I follow my reference for general shapes, but I don't replicate what I see exactly. Loose, spontaneous brushwork suggests detail, such as the rippling pool. This gives the scene a painterly feel that the photograph lacks.

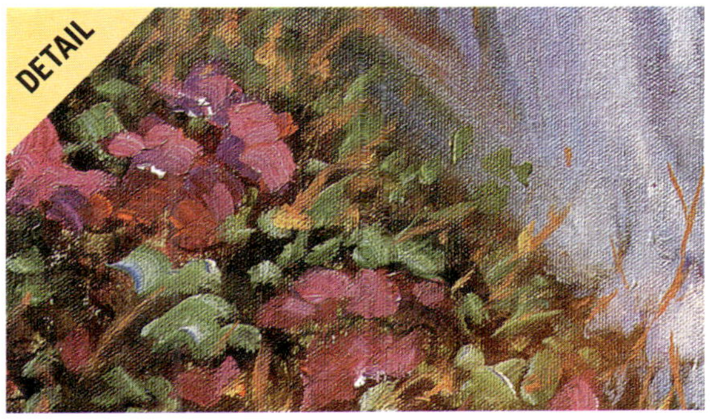

◄ NOTING THE DETAILS For the flowers, I apply Naples yellow mixed with light portrait pink and magenta. A photograph won't always capture color—such as the brilliant magenta of these tropical flowers—the way you see it in person, so you may want to take notes while you're on location.

Determining a Format

Format refers to the shape, size, and orientation of a painting—whether it be rectangular or square, large or small, horizontal or vertical. Often the subject itself will determine the format of a scene. For example, a horizontal format is a logical choice for a broad seascape or landscape, whereas a vertical format is better suited for tall subjects, such as high-rise buildings, a narrow tree, or a standing figure. Horizontal formats are best for showcasing a sweeping, dramatic view of a scene, whereas vertical formats can provide a more intimate, personal focus. You may want to try sketching your subject in several different formats to decide which one you prefer before you begin painting. You can also use a viewfinder to compare different formats, framing your scene before you begin painting. For this painting of a hillside in Lake Como, Italy, I chose a vertical composition. To enhance the intimacy of my format choice, I also crop out the "extra" sky and foreground from my reference photo, which results in a more up-close-and-personal point of view.

Using a Viewfinder

If you have a hard time deciding what area of your scene to zoom in on, try looking through a viewfinder. You can form a double "L" with your fingers or use a cardboard frame, as shown below, and look through the opening. Bring the viewfinder closer and hold it out farther; move it around the scene; look at your subject from high and low viewpoints; and make the opening wider and narrower. Then choose the view that pleases you most.

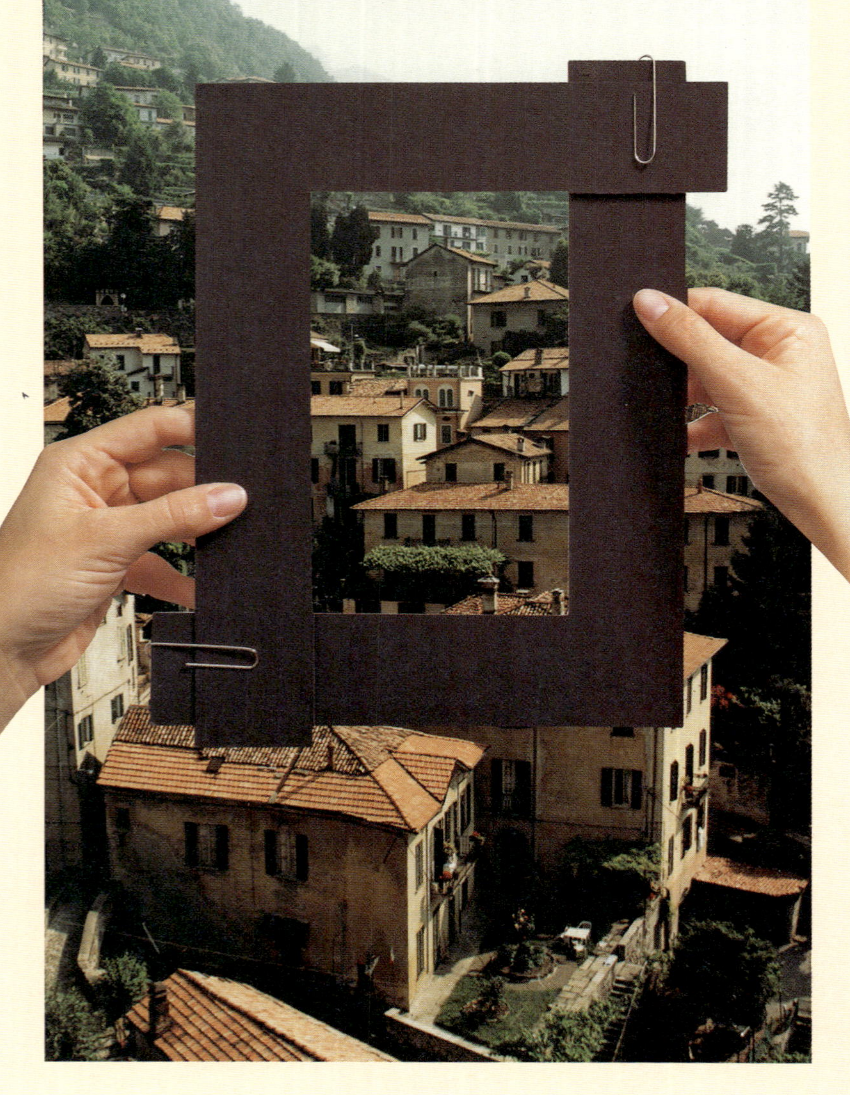

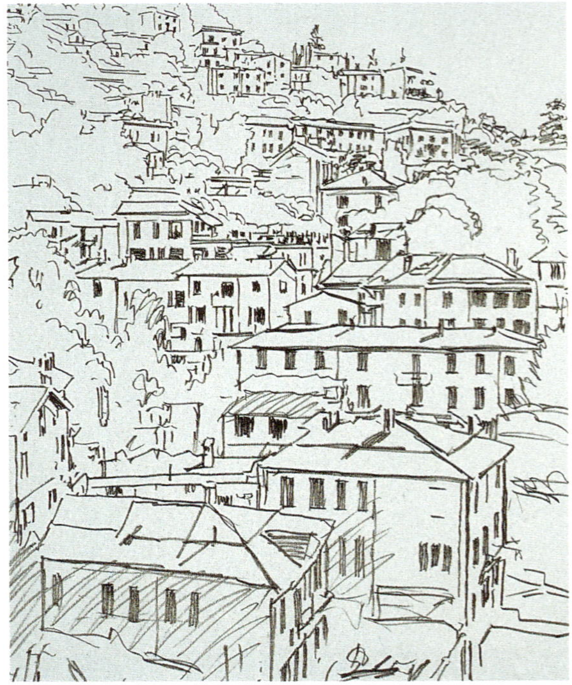

1 Rather than faithfully following my photo reference, I've decided to crop out the foreground of the piece for a stronger, more proportionate composition. I loosely sketch the changed scene on a 30" x 24" stretched canvas, paying careful attention to the perspective but only loosely rendering the details.

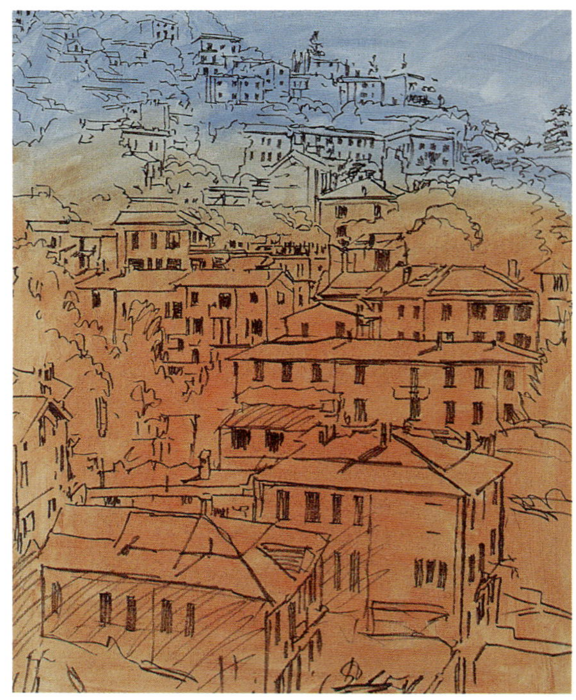

2 To begin the painting, I start with a thin wash that gives me a sense of the value range of warm colors in the foreground to the cooler colors in the distance. I start with only two colors—cerulean blue and burnt sienna. I thin the paint with gloss medium and a little water, and then I use a very large flat sable brush to cover the canvas with large, sweeping strokes. I blend the colors slightly where they meet, giving me a visual guideline for where the value transitions will occur.

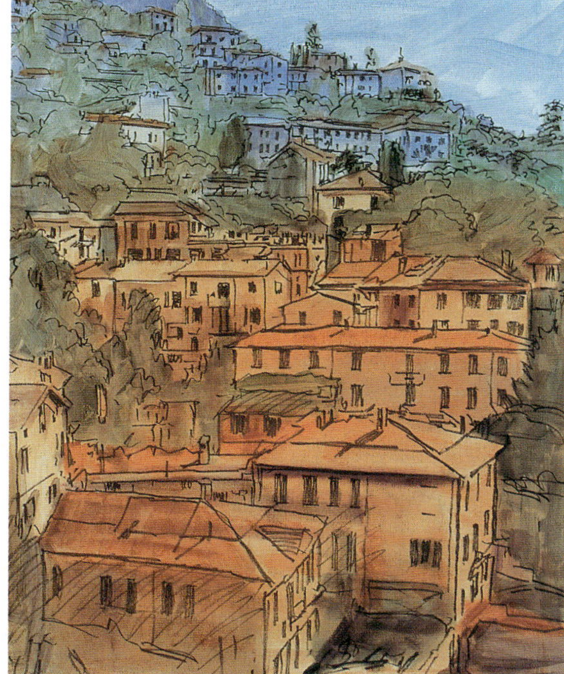

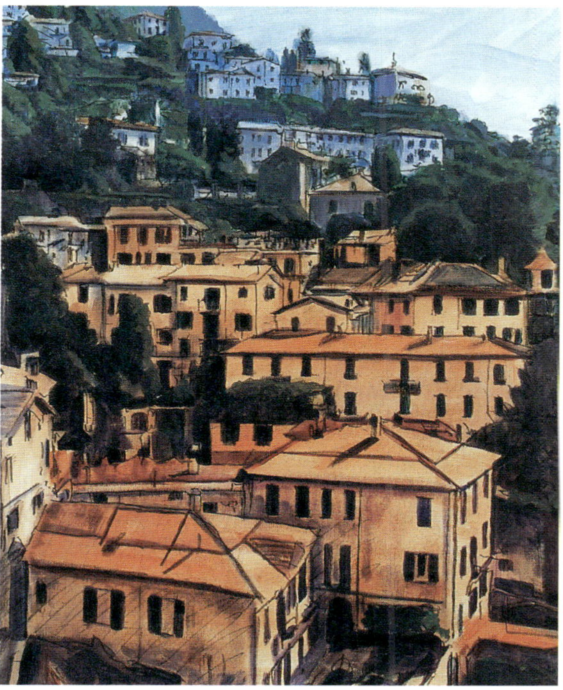

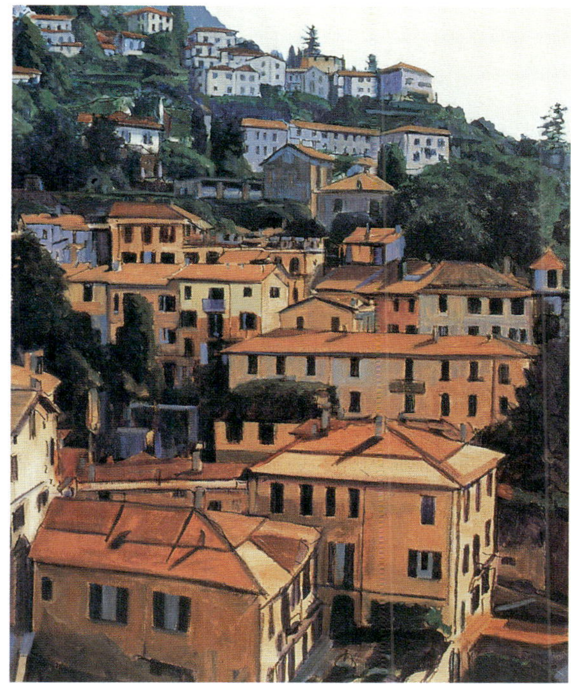

3 Next I apply a mix of sap green, Payne's gray, and dioxazine purple to the foliage. Then I layer burnt sienna on the foreground buildings. I distinguish the shadows with dioxazine purple, which I also apply to the background buildings and rooftops in the distance.

4 I develop the architecture with a dark mix of Prussian blue, phthalo green, and alizarin crimson, adding water for lighter values. I shape the foliage with variations of emerald and permanent green mixed with a little dioxazine purple and Payne's gray. For distant foliage, I add purple and blue.

5 I add mixes of burnt sienna, yellow oxide, magenta, diox. purple, and gloss to the buildings. I mix lt. portrait pink and unbleached titanium for the sky. With lt. blue-violet, lt. portrait pink, and yellow oxide, I paint around the windows, adding touches of lt. blue-violet mixed with diox. purple.

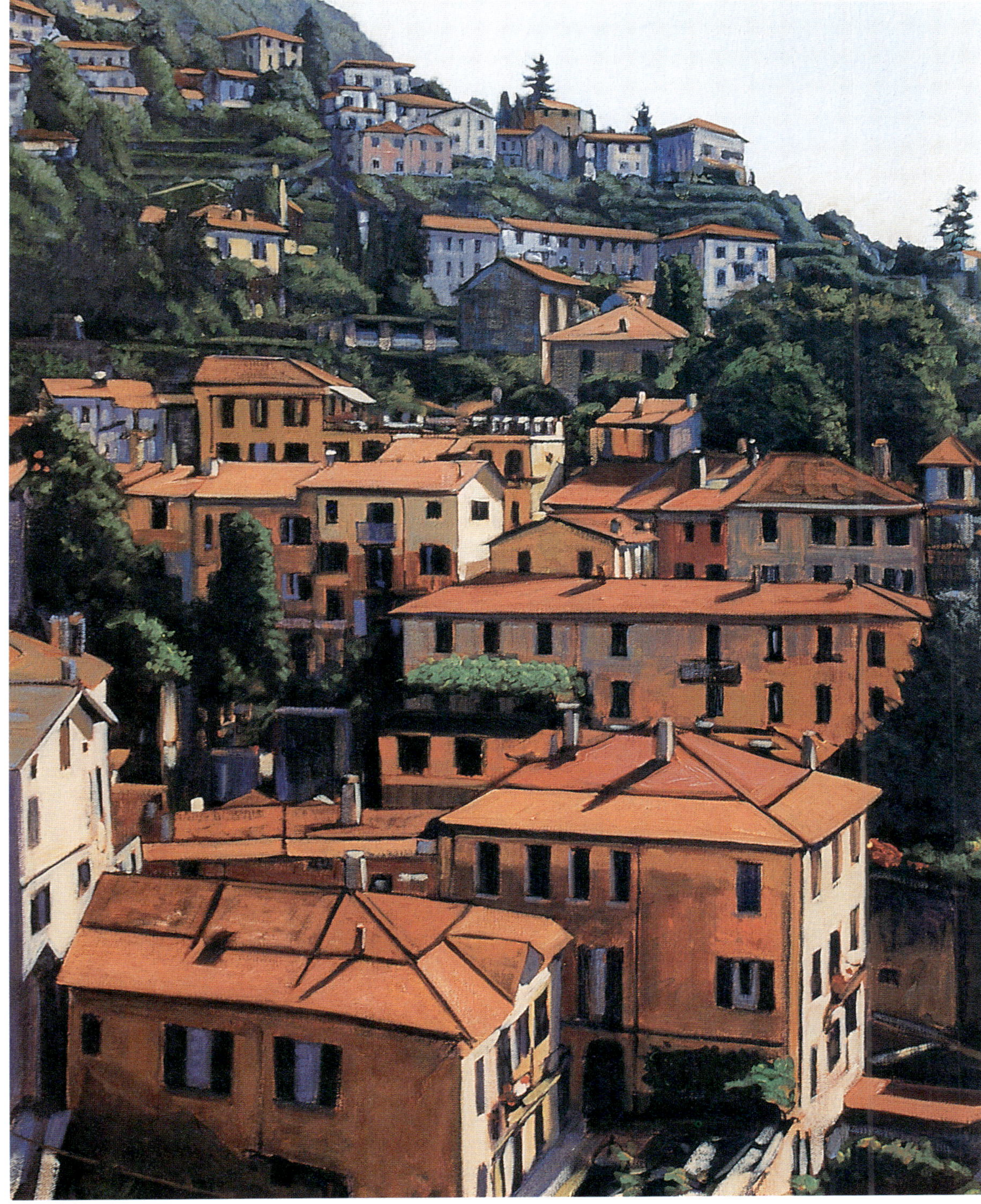

6 To brighten foliage highlights, I mix a few variations of sap green, chromium oxide green, and bronze yellow. I apply the paint more thickly, using drybrush to create a sense of the transition from light to dark. Next I add color to the foliage shadows using sap green mixed with dioxazine purple. I also add a mix of light blue-violet, white, and gloss to the sky. For highlights in the buildings, I apply light portrait pink mixed with bronze yellow. I add details and highlights to the rooftops by mixing variations of red oxide, light portrait pink, bronze yellow, and chrome orange.

SHADOW VARIATIONS

*Dioxazine purple +
light blue-violet*

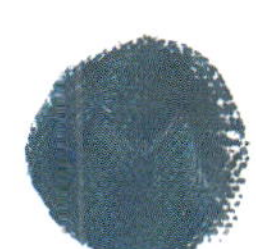

*Cerulean blue +
Payne's gray*

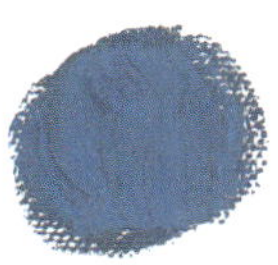

*Light blue-violet +
Payne's gray*

*Dioxazine purple +
unbleached titanium*

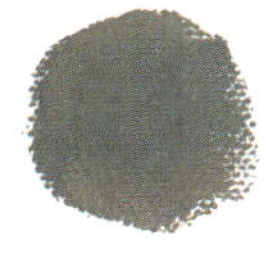

*Payne's gray +
bronze yellow*

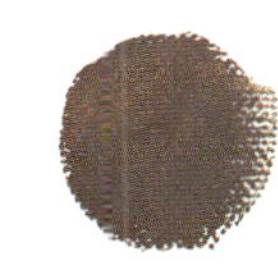

*Red oxide +
unbleached titanium*

Capturing Time of Day

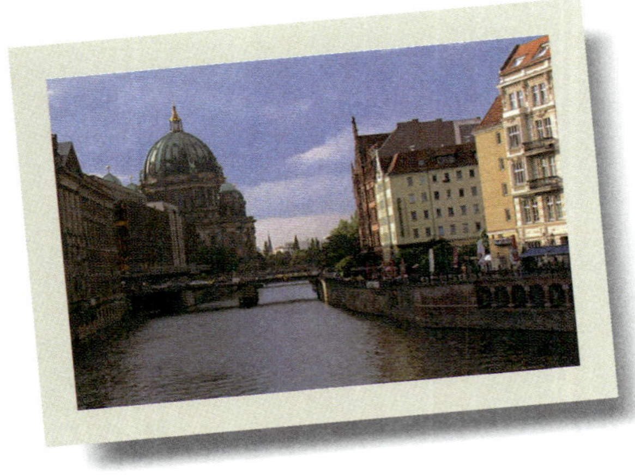

When painting an outdoor scene, time of day becomes a significant factor, since colors, light, and shadows differ at various hours. There are cool hues and longer shadows in the morning and early evening, whereas there are warmer hues and shorter shadows at mid-day. And the warmth or coolness of the colors contributes to the mood your painting will convey. For example, warm, light colors (reds, yellows, and oranges) evoke excitement or passion, whereas cool colors (blues, greens, and violets) have a more calming effect. In this painting of the River Spree in Berlin, the dusky, late-afternoon sun creates long, dramatic shadows and striking contrasts between light and dark. These factors contribute to creating a sense of life in an otherwise quiet scene.

WATER REFLECTIONS

Light portrait pink + magenta

Light portrait pink + magenta + light blue-violet

Light portrait pink + magenta + light blue-violet + ultramarine blue

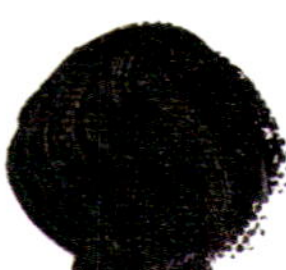

Sap green + dioxazine purple

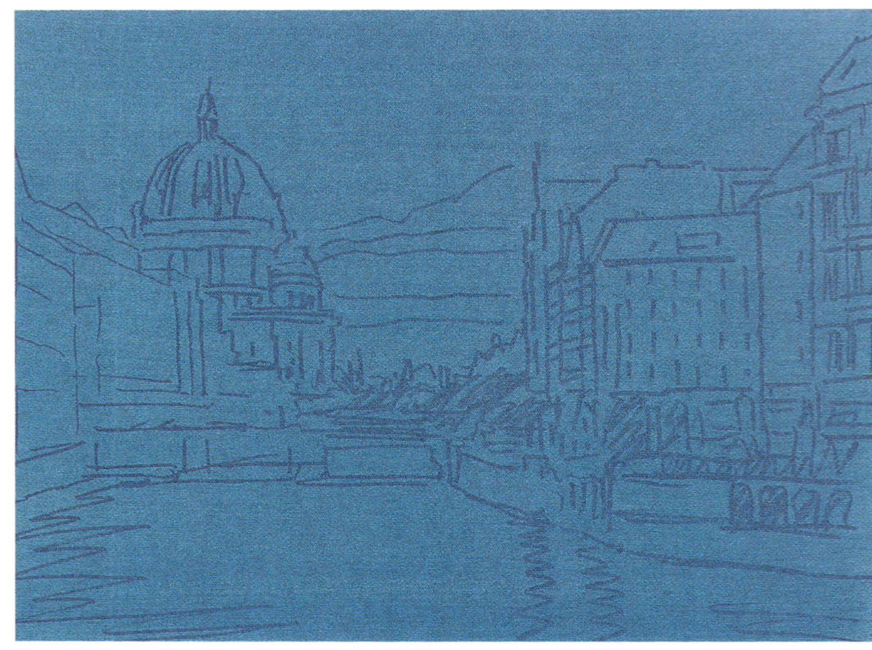

1 First I select a 14" x 18" canvas for my painting, and then I make a very loose sketch with a fine-line black marker before covering the entire canvas with a thin underpainting of cerulean blue.

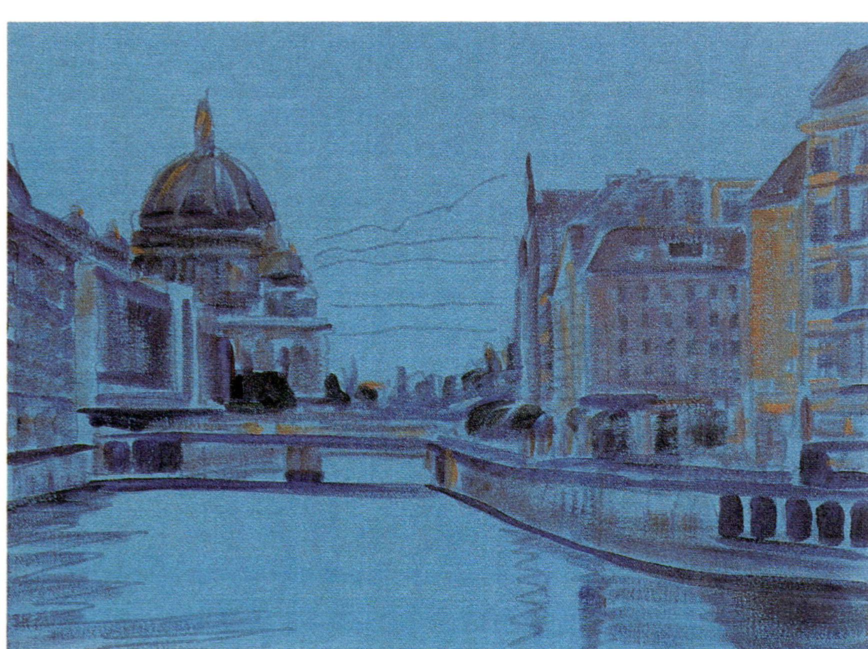

2 Because I want to capture a "plein air" feeling in this work, I mix a gel extender medium with the paint to create a thicker, impasto-type consistency. When I need to vary the thickness of my paints, I just thin them with a little water. To begin, I set up my palette with burnt sienna, raw sienna, ultramarine blue, and Payne's gray. With a large flat brush, I apply basic blocks of color to the canvas, using the edge of the brush to define the shapes.

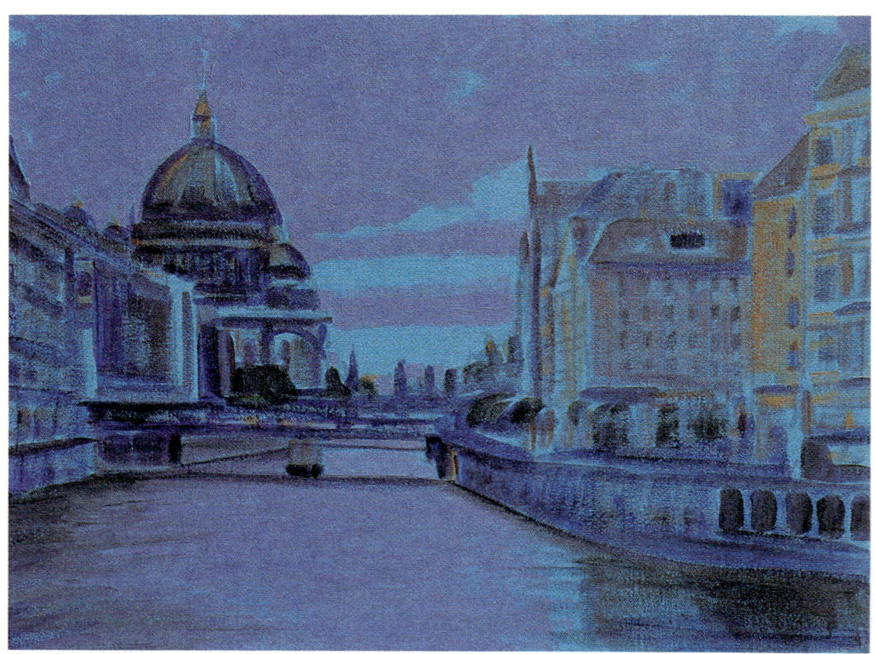

3 For the sky and water, I use Payne's gray mixed with ultramarine blue and light blue-violet, again thickening the paint with gel medium. I keep this underpainting for the sky color, and then I paint the clouds. To darken the reflections along the waterline, I add more Payne's gray to the mix, and I also add dioxazine purple before painting some of the architectural details, such as the outline of the dome.

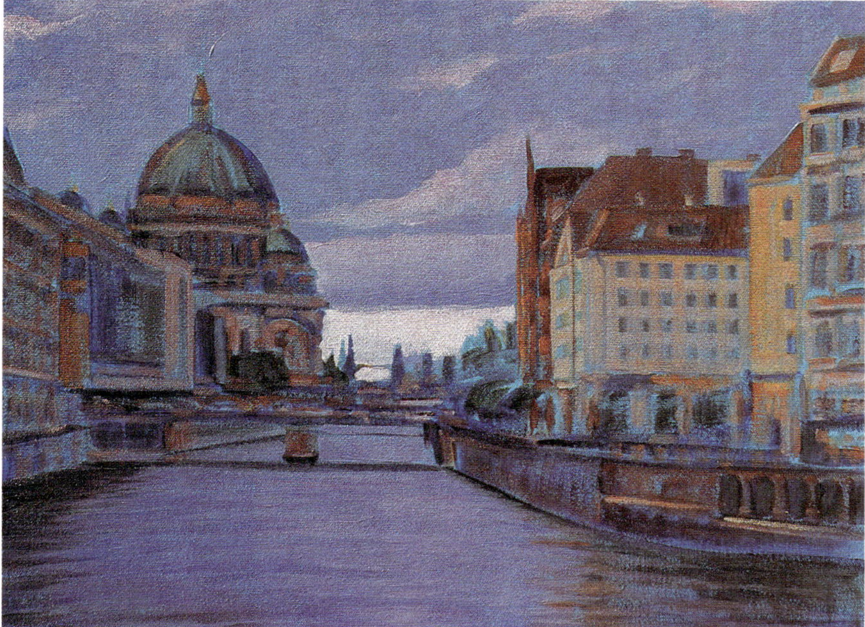

4 Now I add warm mixes of alizarin crimson, burnt sienna, and lt. blue-violet; raw sienna, lt. blue-violet, and Payne's gray; burnt sienna and lt. blue-violet; and dioxazine purple, lt. blue-violet, and Payne's gray. I also apply reflections (see color samples on page 16) using lighter mixes for sky highlights and adding ultramarine blue in the shadows. For the water, I stroke horizontally, and I adjust the water's edge with a mix of dioxazine purple and sap green.

EXPLORING THE SUN'S EFFECT

The strength and position of the sun have a strong influence on outdoor scenes, producing highlights and shadows that differ according to time of day. For example, subtly changing the color and shadows of a scene can convey a cool morning, a blazing noon, or a warm late afternoon.

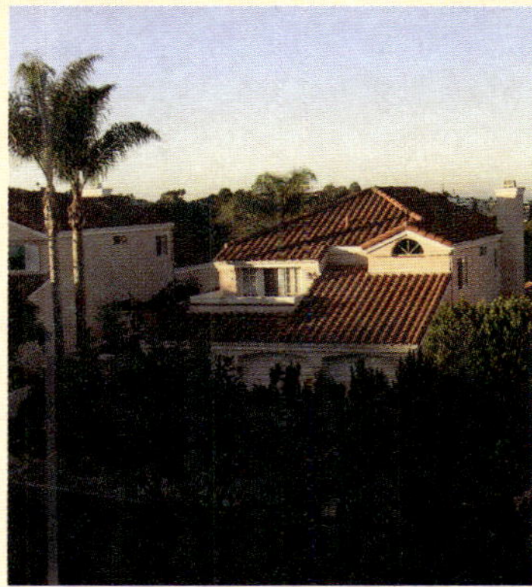
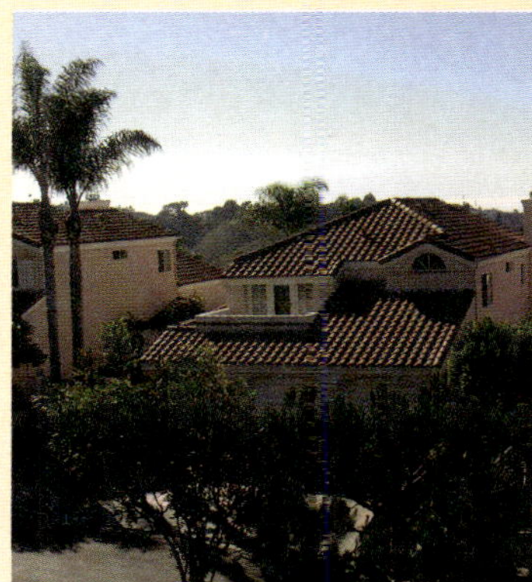

COMPARING TIMES OF DAY The same scene produces two very different impressions in the morning (left) and at mid-day (right). The sun's position affects the colors of the scene and alters the shadows on the tree, roof, and street.

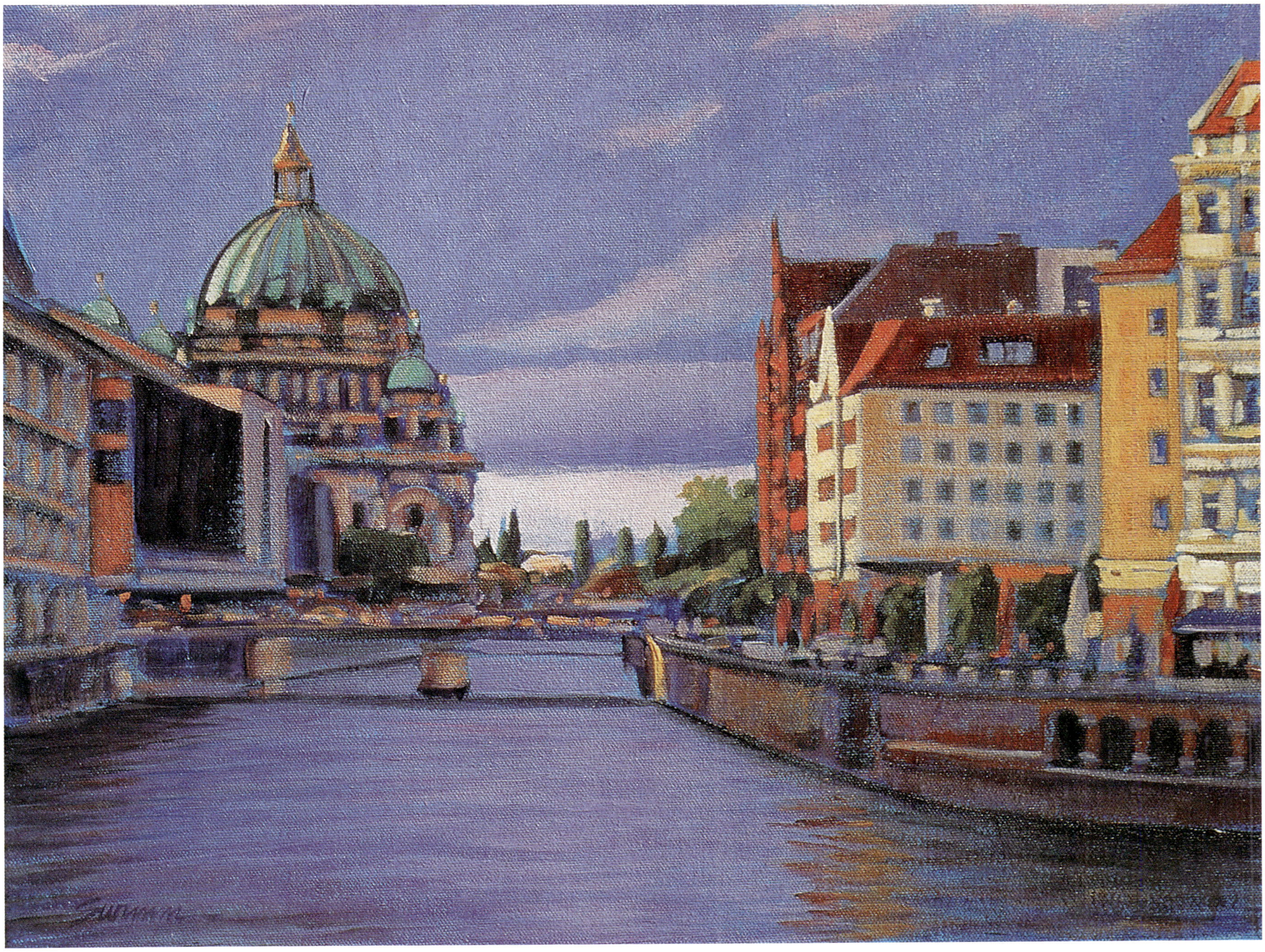

5 For the dome, I use variations of phthalo green mixed with light blue-violet and gel medium. Then, for the distant foliage, I mix sap green, Payne's gray, and burnt sienna, and I apply the color with single brushstrokes. Next I build up the values of the buildings, applying raw sienna mixed with unbleached titanium and light blue-violet, then switching to alizarin crimson mixed with light blue-violet for the roofs. I also apply a few dabs of color to the dome and the façade on the left. Then I work with the water reflections on the right, applying loose, horizontal strokes of alizarin crimson mixed with raw sienna. For highlights on the dome and buildings, I mix titanium white and cadmium yellow light, switching to cadmium red light for roof highlights. I work these colors over the entire canvas, using drybrush in places to suggest detail. Then, to finish, I glaze over the clouds with light blue-violet.

PAINTING STILL WATER

Water reflections are a recurring theme

in my work, and I'm often inspired by the way the movement of the water influences the appearance of a scene. But water can take on many forms—whether calm and still or turbulent and in motion—and the reflections of objects will appear quite different depending on the state of the water. In moving water, reflections are blurred and less distinct. (See "Depicting Moving Water" on page 22.) In water at rest, images are reflected more clearly, yet they still aren't exact mirror images. Even in still water, the colors in the reflections will be a little less intense than they are in the objects themselves; while light-colored objects will appear somewhat darker, dark-colored objects will appear just a bit lighter. And even in very calm water, the object's form won't appear quite as crisp and distinct in the reflection, as can be seen in this scene from Florence, Italy, near the Ponte Vecchio bridge.

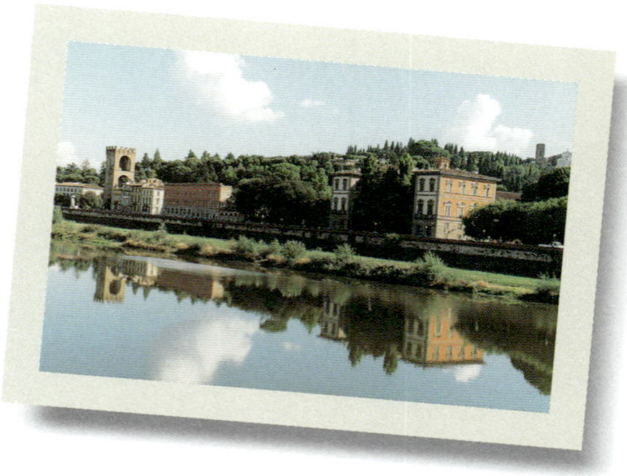

CREATING DRAMA Reflections can add interest and drama to a painting, especially when they're unusually sharp and clear. On this crisp, sunny fall afternoon, there was little wind to disturb the still river, so the colorful, old-world landscape is clearly mirrored in its neighboring waters.

1 For a stronger composition, I decide to alter the image from my reference photo slightly, cropping out a bit of the scene on both the left and right for my sketch. I use a gray marker to draw a loose sketch on the canvas, shading the darkest areas with crisscross strokes.

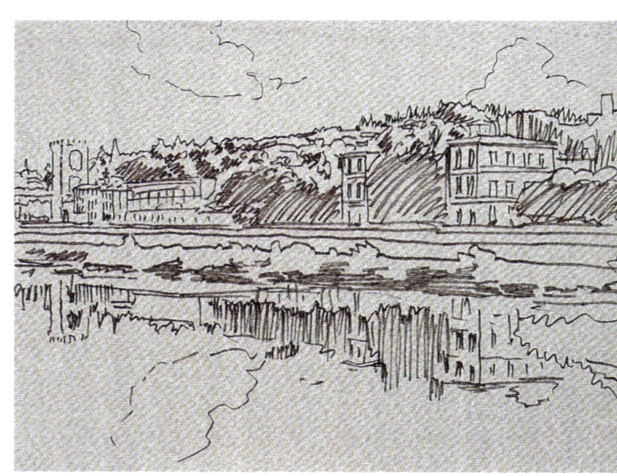

2 Next I apply two underpainting colors: dioxazine purple and chrome orange. These colors provide a clear visual separation of the color values and they also add subtle harmony to the subsequent layers.

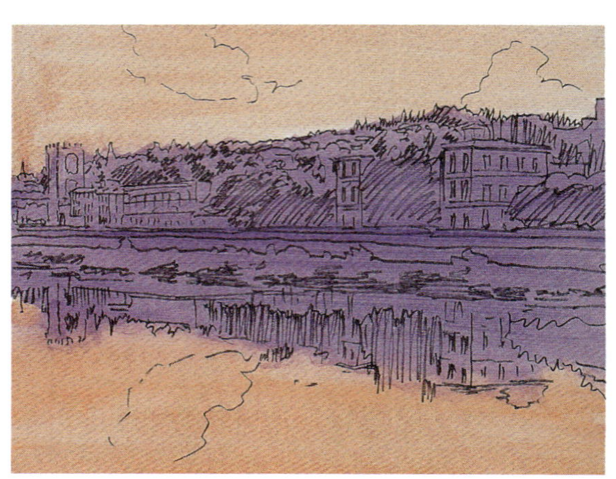

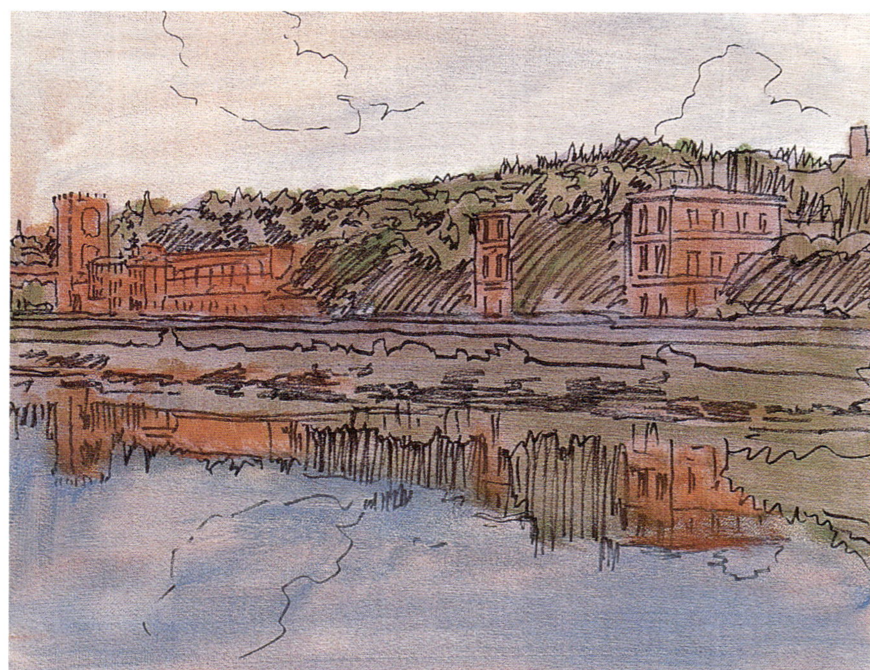

3 I block in transparent washes with dioxazine purple, Payne's gray, sap green, cerulean blue, red oxide, and yellow oxide, mixed with gloss medium. For the dark reflections of the trees and buildings, I add a little Payne's gray to the pure color. And I use stronger color (with less medium) to darken the sky's reflection. (Remember: In reflections, light colors appear slightly darker and dark colors appear a bit lighter.)

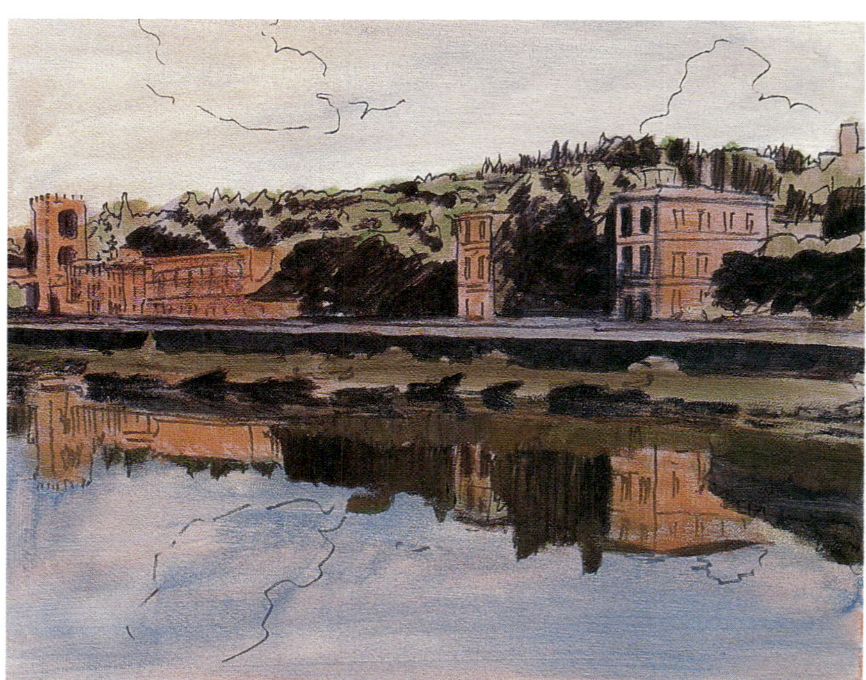

4 Next I move on to the darker values, using mixtures of sap green, burnt sienna, Payne's gray, and dioxazine purple to paint the scene above water. I want these layers to be a bit more opaque than previous applications, so I mix them with just a little gel medium. Then, to establish the reflections, I pull the color down with vertical strokes into the water. Next I define the edges of the buildings and windows using a small flat sable brush.

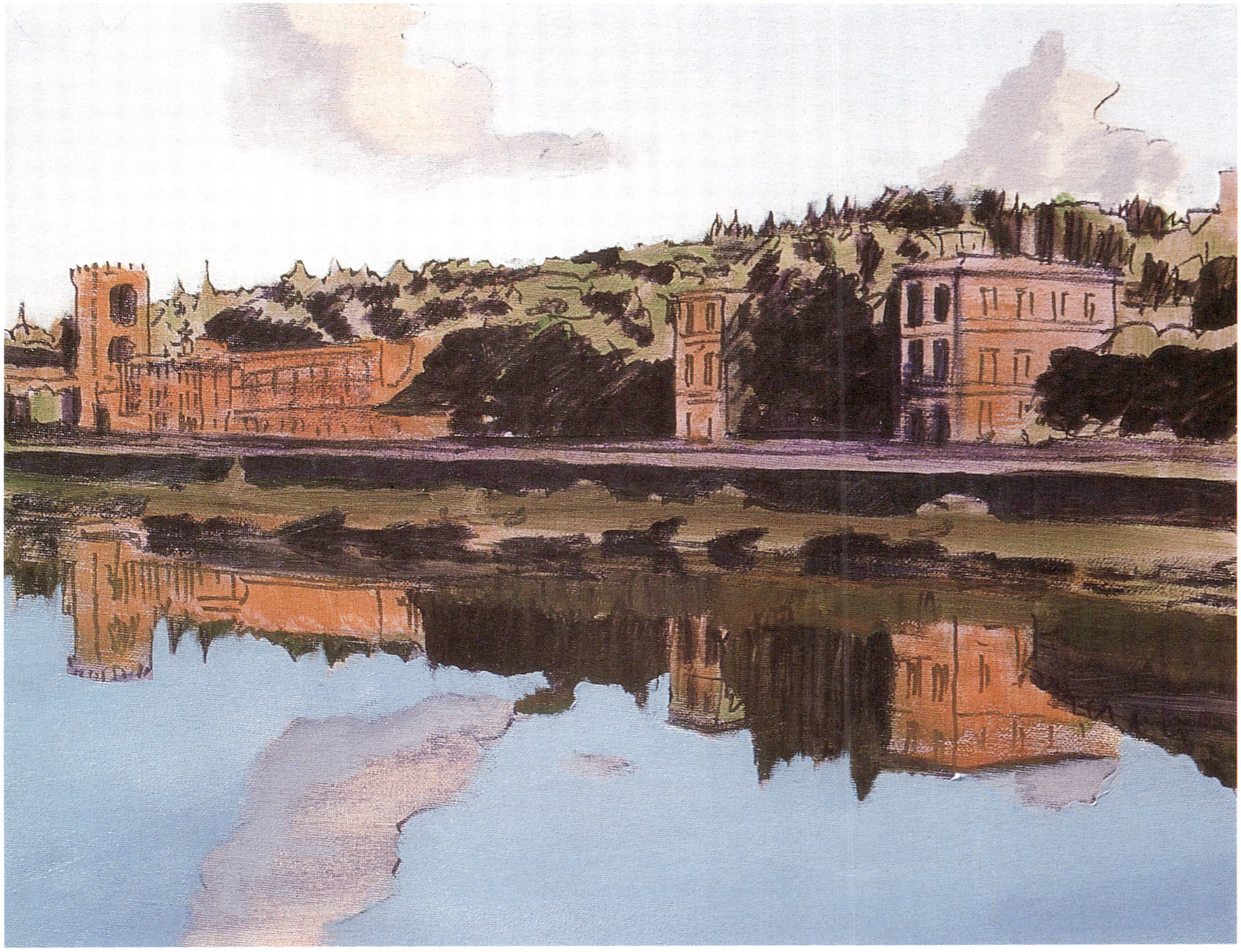

5 I add another layer
of color to the sky
and water, mixing white,
cerulean blue, and gel
medium for a thicker
application. Because the
reflected sky is darker than
the real sky, I use a little
more cerulean blue in the
reflection mix. For the
clouds, I apply light blue-
violet mixed with a little
dioxazine purple, and I
soften the edges using a
drybrush technique.

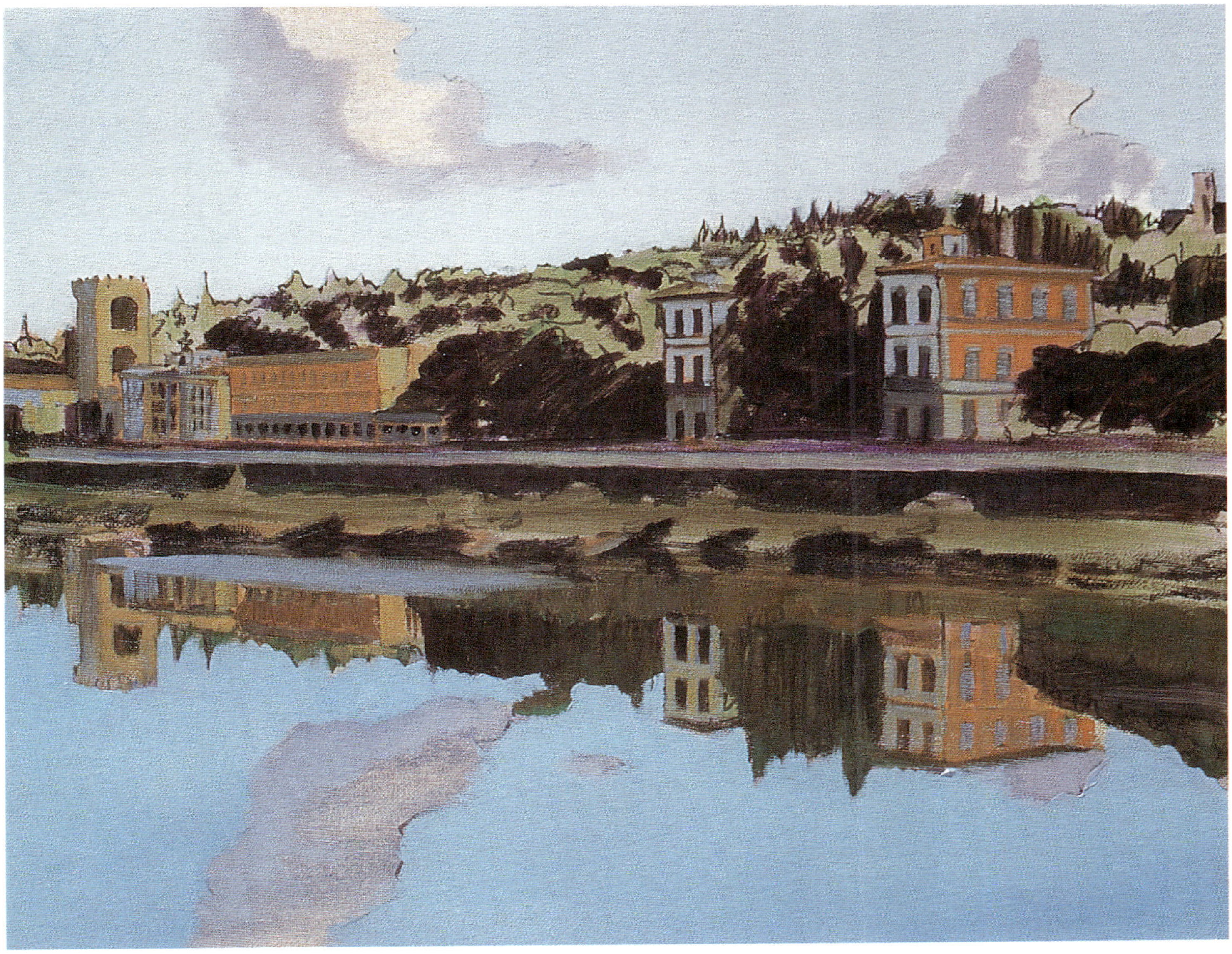

6 With the red oxide,
yellow oxide, and light
blue-violet already on my
palette, I mix a few color
variations to define the
building details. I also add
a bluish highlight to the
water on the left, applying
dioxazine purple mixed
with light blue-violet using
a dry brush and horizontal
brushstrokes.

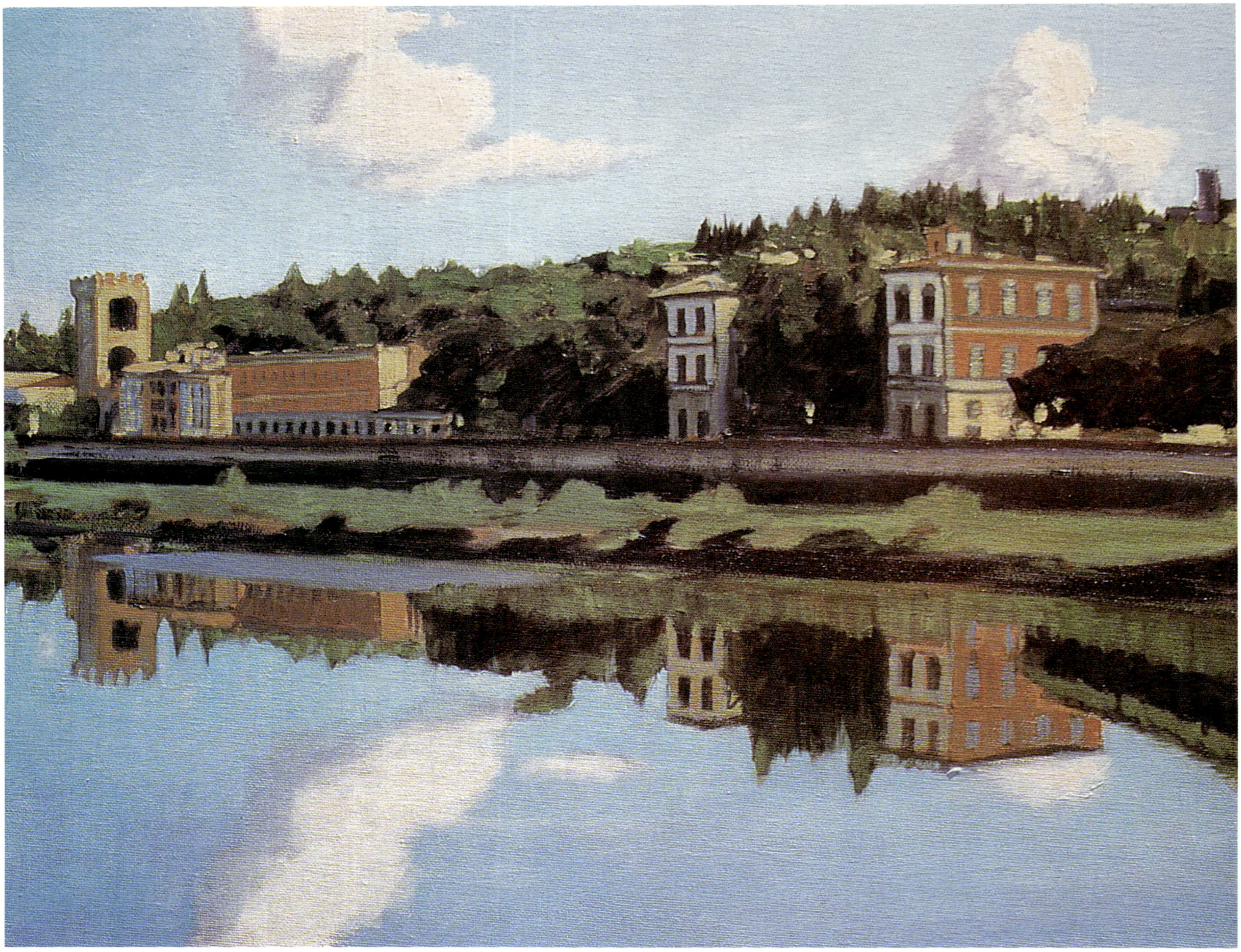

7 Next I mix some variations of sap green, chromium oxide green, cerulean blue, Payne's gray, and yellow oxide to develop detail and add color variation to the trees and foliage. I mix gel medium into the colors to thicken the paint, and then I apply the colors using a large flat sable brush and varying the direction of the brushstrokes to define the different shapes of the trees. Applying atmospheric perspective (see page 8), I keep the darker colors in the distance, adding gradually lighter colors as I move forward. I also add another layer of highlights to the clouds, this time using light portrait pink mixed with unbleached titanium. For harmony, I apply the same color to the brightest areas of the buildings.

PAINTING UPSIDE-DOWN

You may find it helpful to turn your painting upside-down when it comes time to paint the reflections. This way you can focus on rendering the buildings, foliage, and architecture in the same manner you did for the reflected objects, without having to reorient your viewpoint.

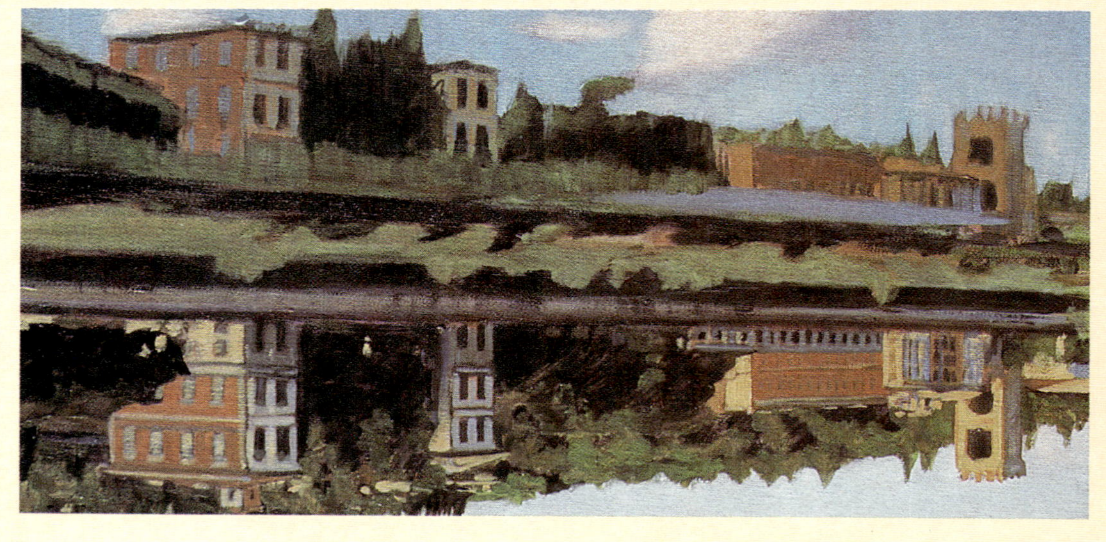

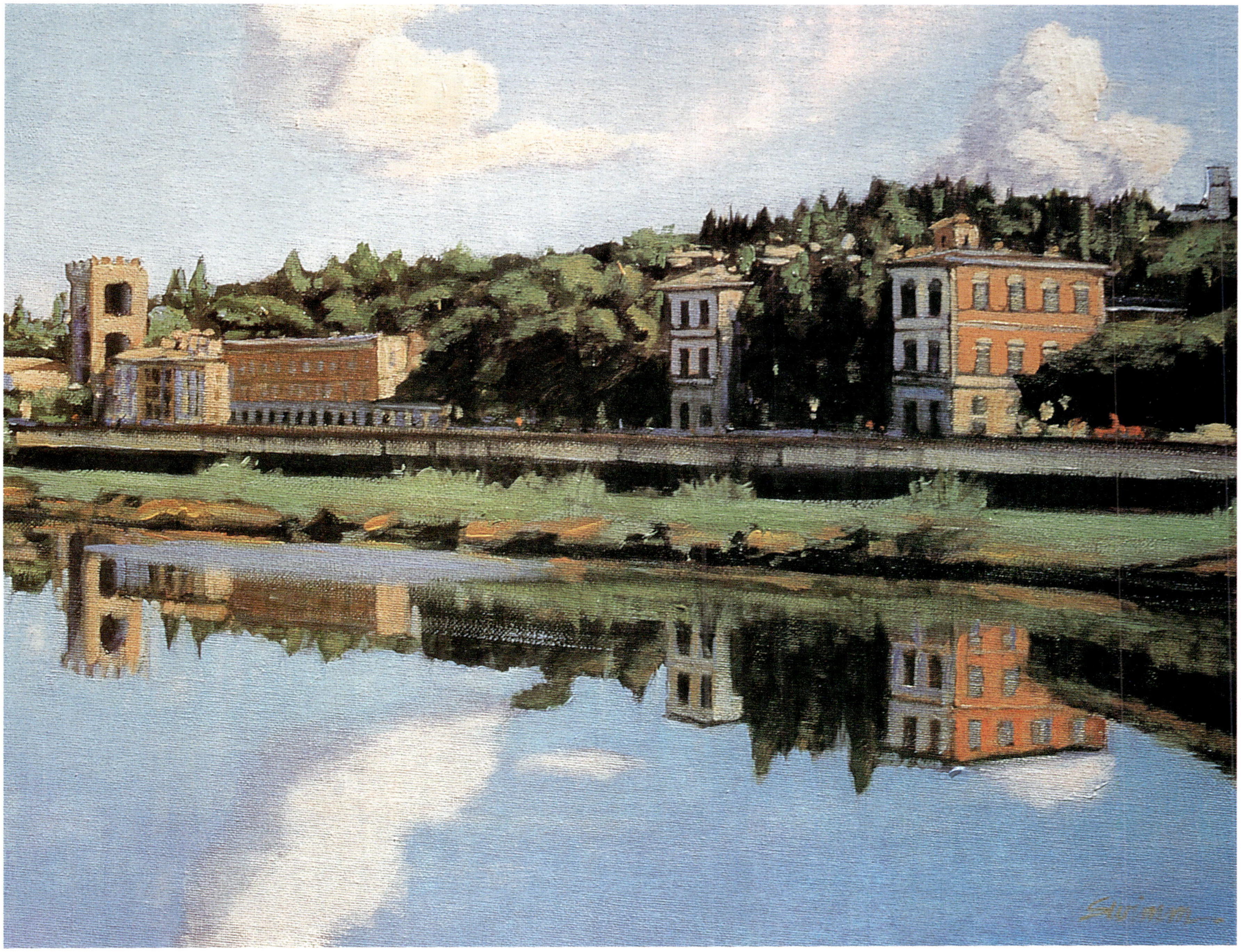

8 Now it's time to make a few final adjustments. First I brighten the foliage with mixtures of yellow oxide, titanium white, and chromium oxide green. I also apply a few random strokes of yellow oxide mixed with chrome orange along the shoreline. Next, to brighten the building colors, I make a few more suggestions of detail, dabbing on small spots of the color mixes I've used earlier. Although this painting is realistic and has its fair share of detail, there's no need to render every aspect of the painting exactly and minutely. Little flecks of color here and there can give the impression of windows, lampposts, or even figures along the walkway.

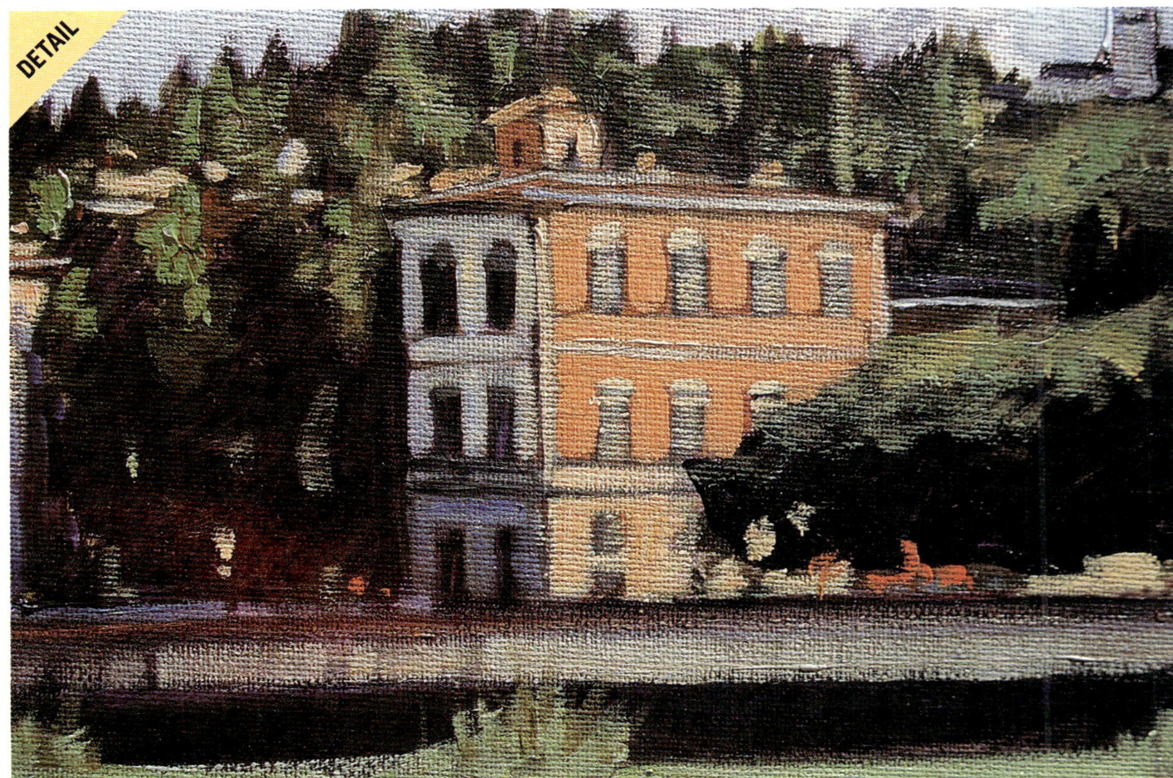

◄ ADDING FINAL HIGHLIGHTS For the final highlights, I've used colors already on my palette to harmonize the scene. I touch up the windows on the right side of the building with short horizontal strokes, leaving dark colors evident to give the appearance of reflected light. And I clarify the direction of the light source by placing the brightest highlights in the direct path of the sun, which is coming from above right.

DEPICTING MOVING WATER

As you've already discovered, when you're depicting still water, the reflections will be almost the same size and shape as the subject being reflected. (See "Painting Still Water" on page 18.) But, in moving water, the ripples and waves will lengthen and distort the reflected image. Keep in mind the direction of the movement of the water as you paint. The water's ripples have a definite curvature, and your brushstrokes should always follow the flow of the water, even in the reflections. Also, as with still water, the colors of the reflected object are slightly muted. And in shallow water, the bottom surface color will influence the reflected colors as well, as can be seen in this scene from Berlin.

► **INCLUDING UNUSUAL ELEMENTS** Although some may think it mars the scene, I decide to keep the bridge in the foreground, as I like the way it frames the composition. Including an unusual visual element like this can add interest and character to a scene.

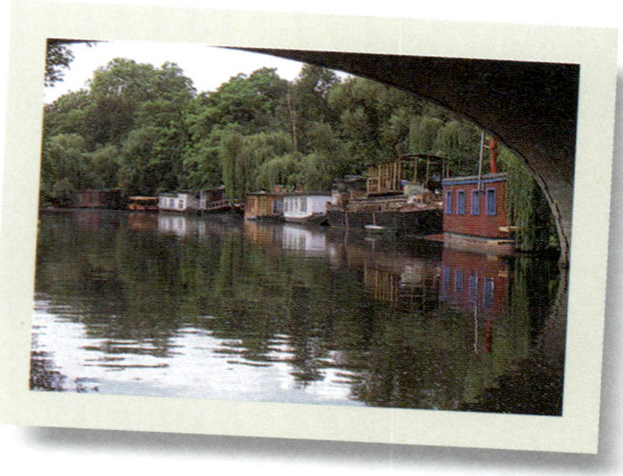

FINAL HOUSEBOAT DETAILS

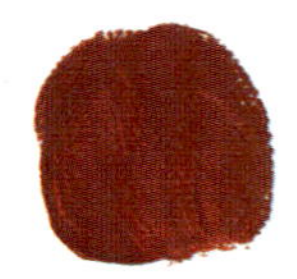

Alizarin crimson + red oxide

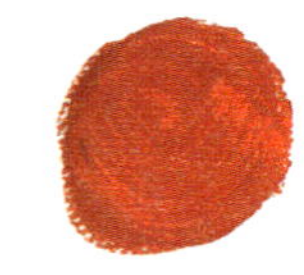

Cadmium red light + cadmium yellow light

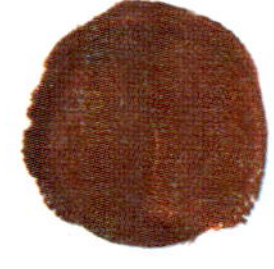

Burnt sienna + cadmium red light

FINAL FOLIAGE DETAILS

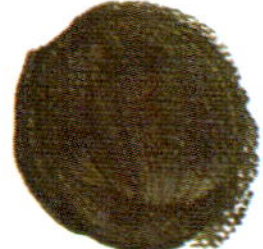

Sap green + bronze yellow

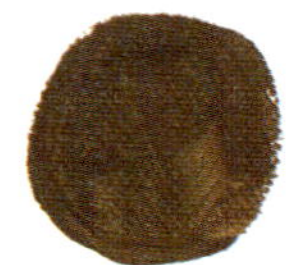

Sap green + raw sienna

Dioxazine purple + light blue-violet + burnt sienna

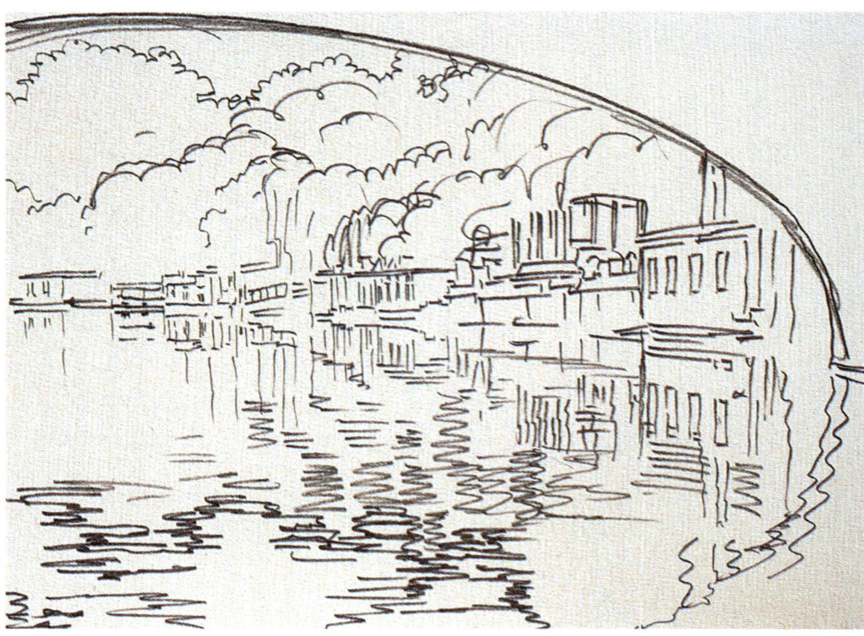

1 Using my photo as a reference, I make a very quick and simple sketch on the canvas to begin. I add a few rough indications of the ripples and movement in the water, but I don't concern myself with too much detail at this stage.

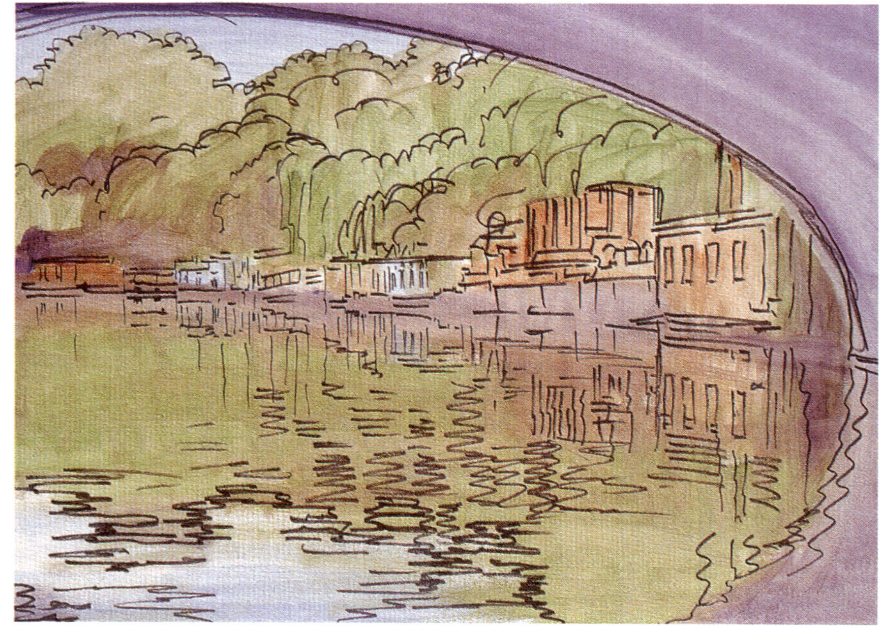

2 To separate the visual elements, I block in large areas of color. I apply the water-thinned paint with a medium round bristle brush, keeping the paint application transparent and free-flowing. For the trees and their reflections, I apply sap green; for the bridge and shadow areas, I use dioxazine purple. I paint some of the houseboats with burnt sienna and switch to light blue-violet for the remaining houseboats, the sky, and the water.

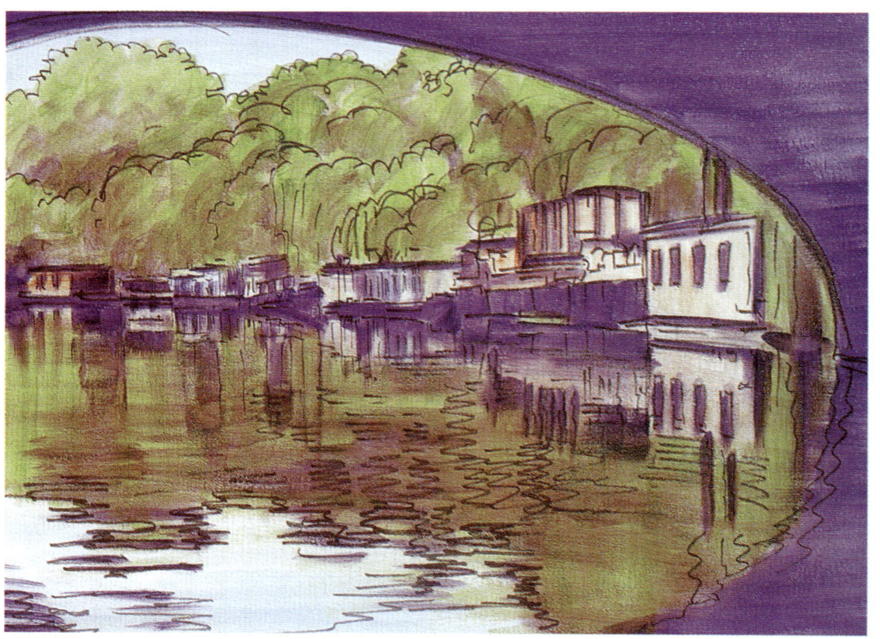

3 With more opaque paint and a large flat bristle brush, I layer dioxazine purple on the bridge's underside, creating its reflection with horizontal strokes. I also use purple to define details on the houseboats, adding burnt sienna for variation. Then I apply more sap green to the trees, using purple for shadows. I use the same colors for reflections, mixing in gloss medium and pulling the paint first down and then across to simulate the water.

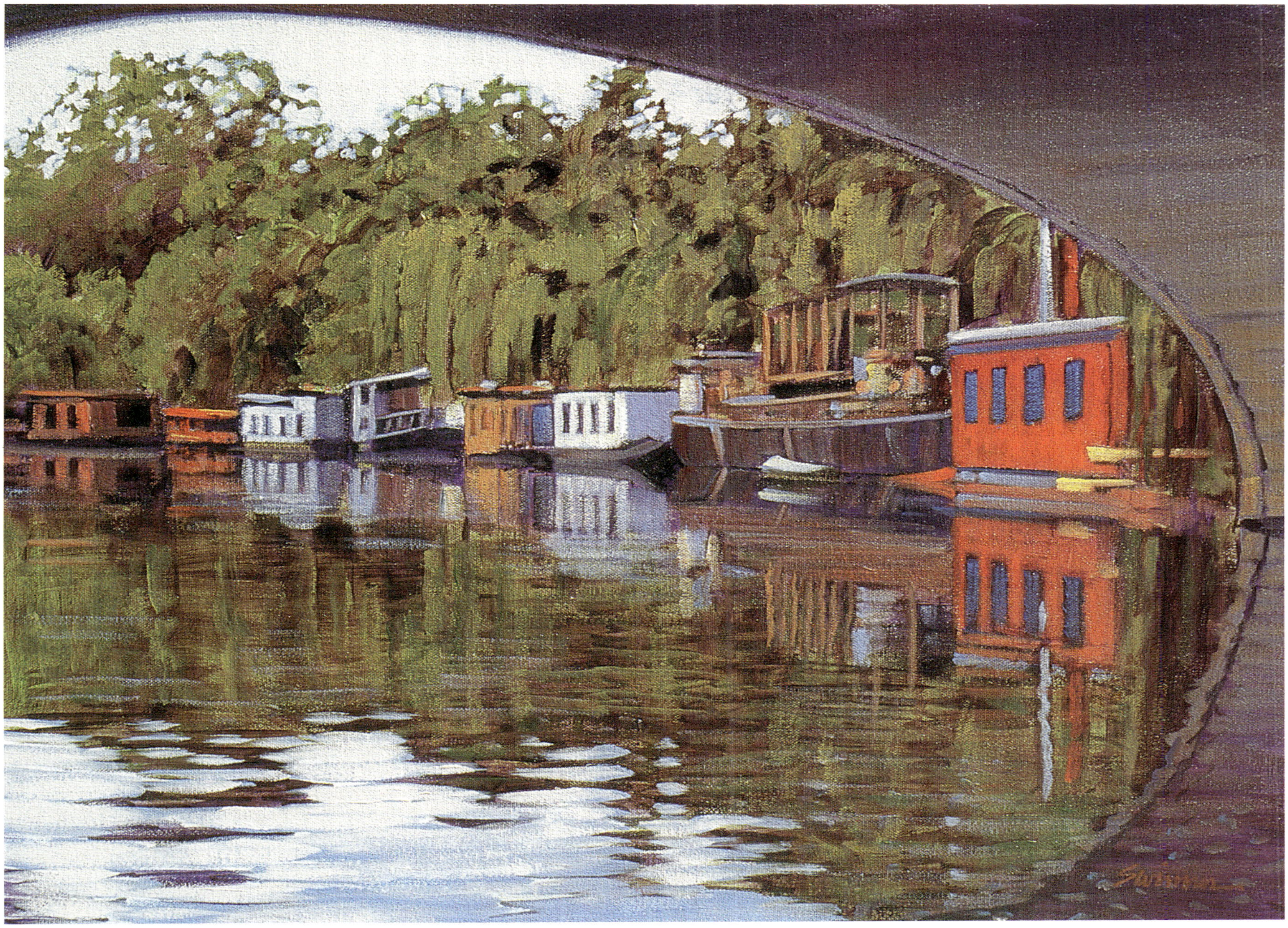

6 Next, with a mixture of dioxazine purple, burnt sienna, and light blue-violet, I apply an opaque layer of paint over the bridge and its reflection, blending the paint while it's still wet to create a gradual shading effect. In the foreground water, I add a few horizontal lines with burnt sienna and apply light blue-violet to suggest leaves. To add detail to the foliage, I loosely brush on various thick mixtures of raw sienna, bronze yellow, and sap green. In the shadows, I add dioxazine purple to the mixes. And I use the same colors for the tree reflec-

tions. I also add another layer of color to the sky, this time using light portrait pink mixed with light blue-violet. I apply the same mixture to the reflections on the water, allowing some of the blue underpainting to peek through. To finish the houseboats, I add a few more colors to the palette—red oxide, cadmium yellow light, and cadmium red light. With these colors (see color samples on page 22) and the edge of a medium flat sable brush, I detail the houseboats and then render their reflections using drybrush.

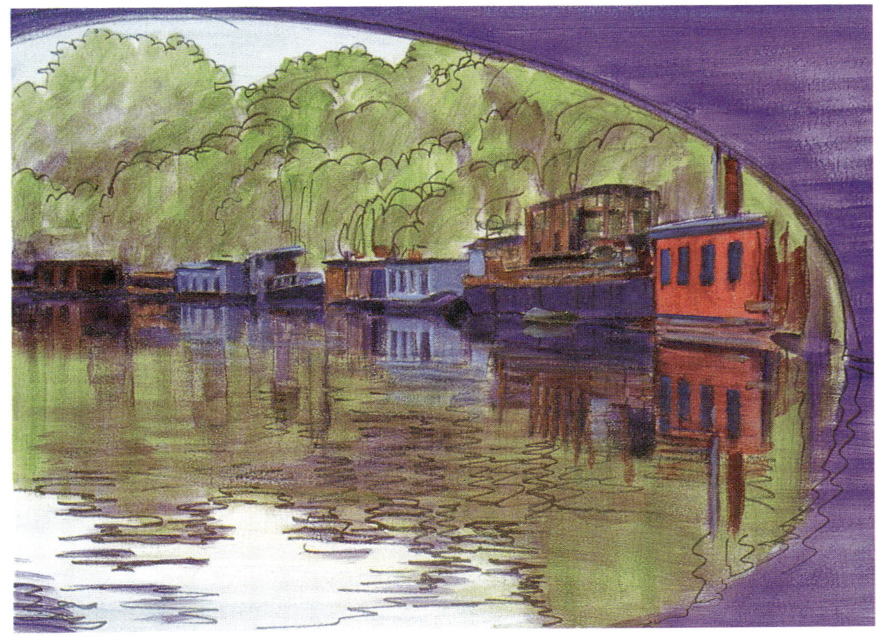

4 Next I introduce more color to the houseboats. Using the photo as a color reference, I add ultramarine blue and alizarin crimson to my palette; then I switch to a smaller medium flat brush to apply the color, "drawing" in the detail. Remember to keep the symmetry between the boats and their reflections consistent—whatever is painted above the water line should also be placed below.

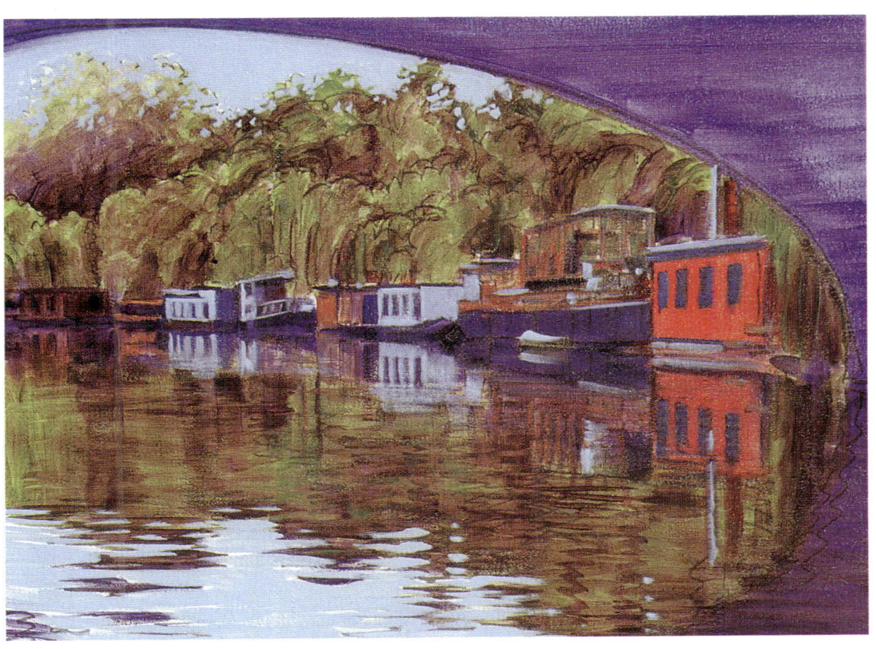

5 Now I further darken and define the foliage, pulling the color down, then across for the reflections. Next I paint the sky and water with light blue-violet, applying the paint more thickly to cover the drawing. To define the edge of the tree line and the ripples in the water, I paint the negative space using light blue-violet mixed with unbleached titanium. Then I apply the same color to a few of the houseboats, drybrushing the paint on the reflections.

RENDERING NIGHT SCENES

People often associate night scenes with darkness and mystery, calling to mind a dim moonlit lake or an overcast evening sky. But night scenes don't have to be sinister or foreboding; they can also be warm and intimate. For example, lamps or candles can emit a warm glow against the backdrop of night, reflecting onto neighboring walls and spilling onto the streets to produce a cozy, welcoming scene. Night scenes also appear more inviting when they include colorful elements—such as the red tablecloths featured in this café located in the Plaka section of Athens. Lively characters round out the setting, breathing life into the night scene.

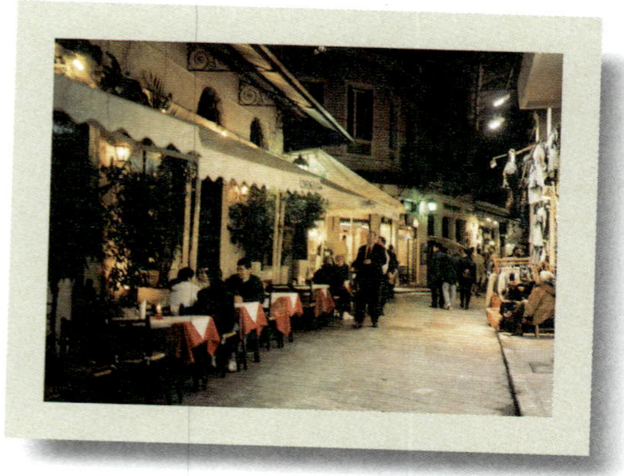

CREATING INTIMACY Night scenes have an intimacy to them unmatched by most daytime subjects. To enhance that sense of closeness, I chose to focus on the figures and activity in the scene, rather than on the buildings.

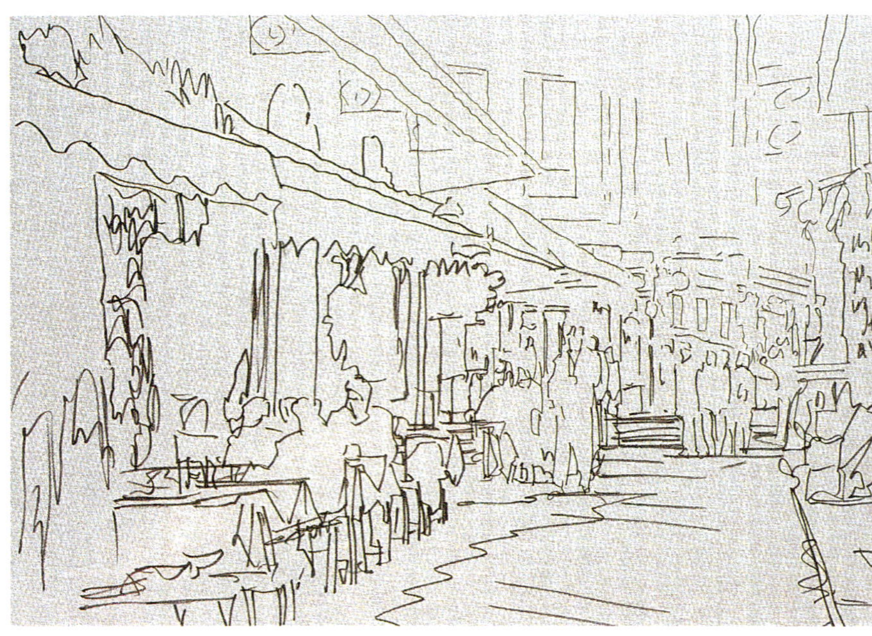

1 I select a relatively small 18" x 24" stretched canvas to enhance the intimate, romantic nature of the scene. Then I make a loose sketch with a fine-line black marker. I keep my drawing very simple, and I don't focus too much on precision, concentrating instead on capturing the basic shapes of the composition.

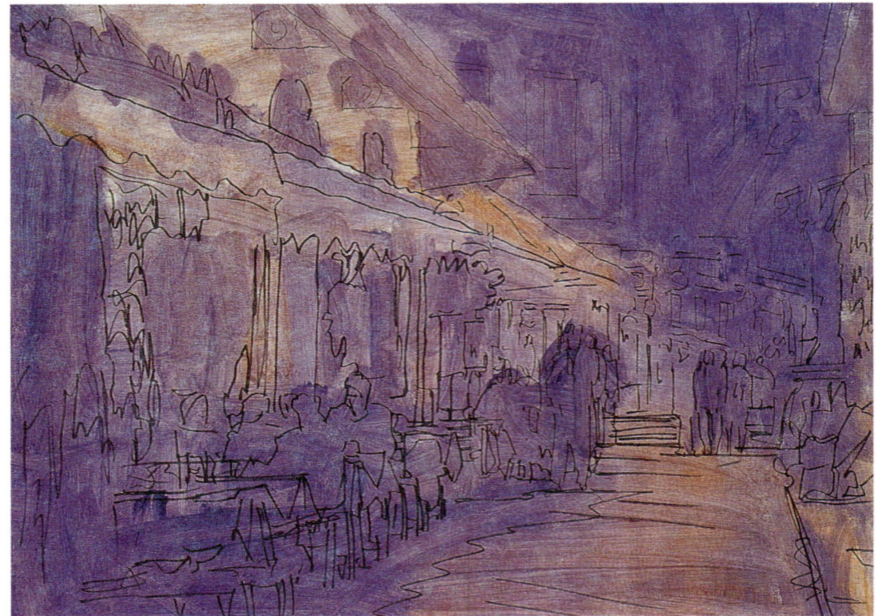

2 To begin, I establish the separation of the light and dark areas with transparent washes of two colors: dioxazine purple and raw sienna. First I mix the paints with gloss medium to make them more fluid. Then I apply the colors with a very large flat brush, using quick, sweeping motions and blending the paint in areas of transition.

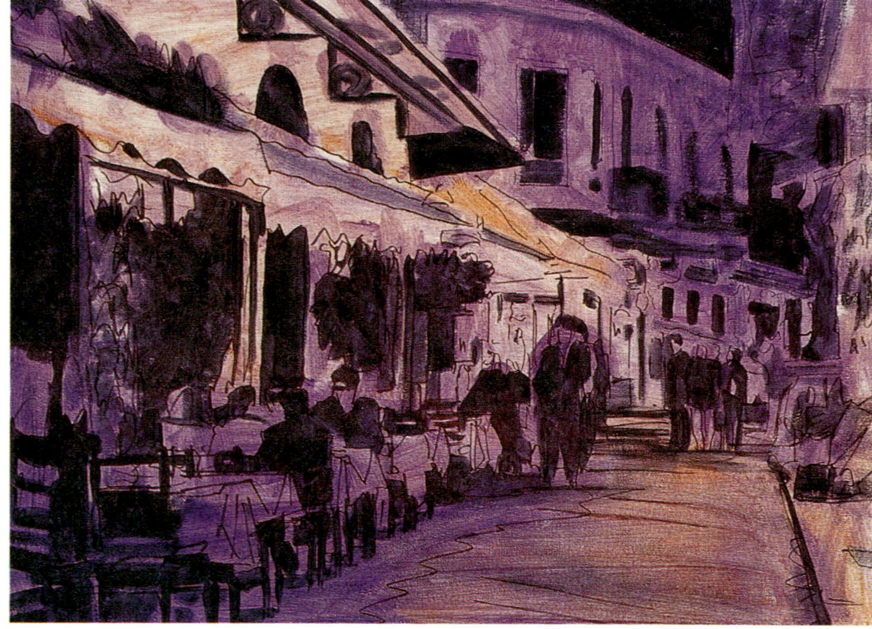

3 When the underpainting is dry, I establish the darkest values, using my sketch as a guide for placement. I fill in the shadow areas with a large flat brush and Payne's gray mixed with sap green and gel medium. Using the edge of the brush makes it easy to draw and define the details, especially on the figures.

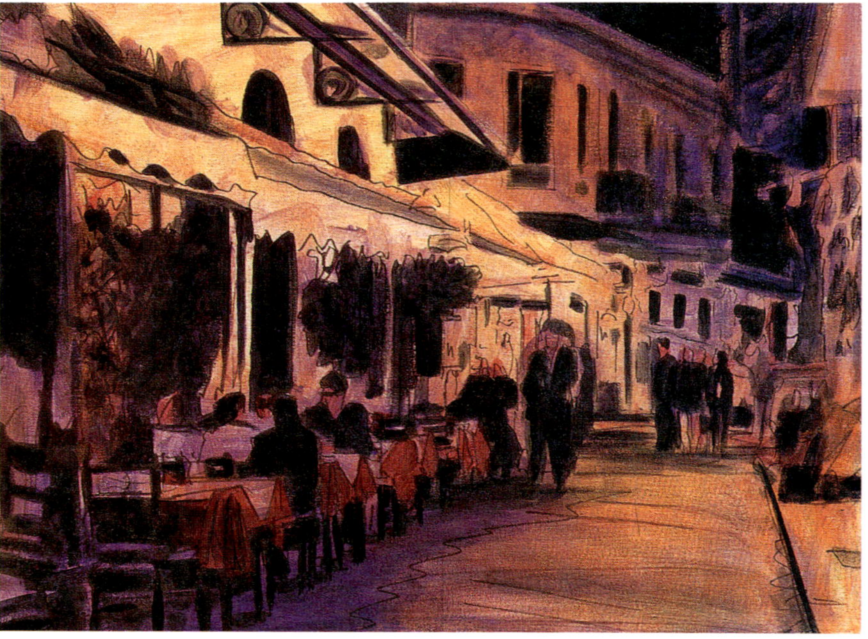

4 Now I apply mixes of yellow oxide, raw sienna, and burnt sienna to the buildings and the street. For harmony, I thin yellow oxide with glazing medium and then glaze over the entire scene, working the paint into the canvas with a large brush to soften the edges. For contrast, I reestablish the darkest values. Then I apply alizarin crimson to the tablecloths and figures.

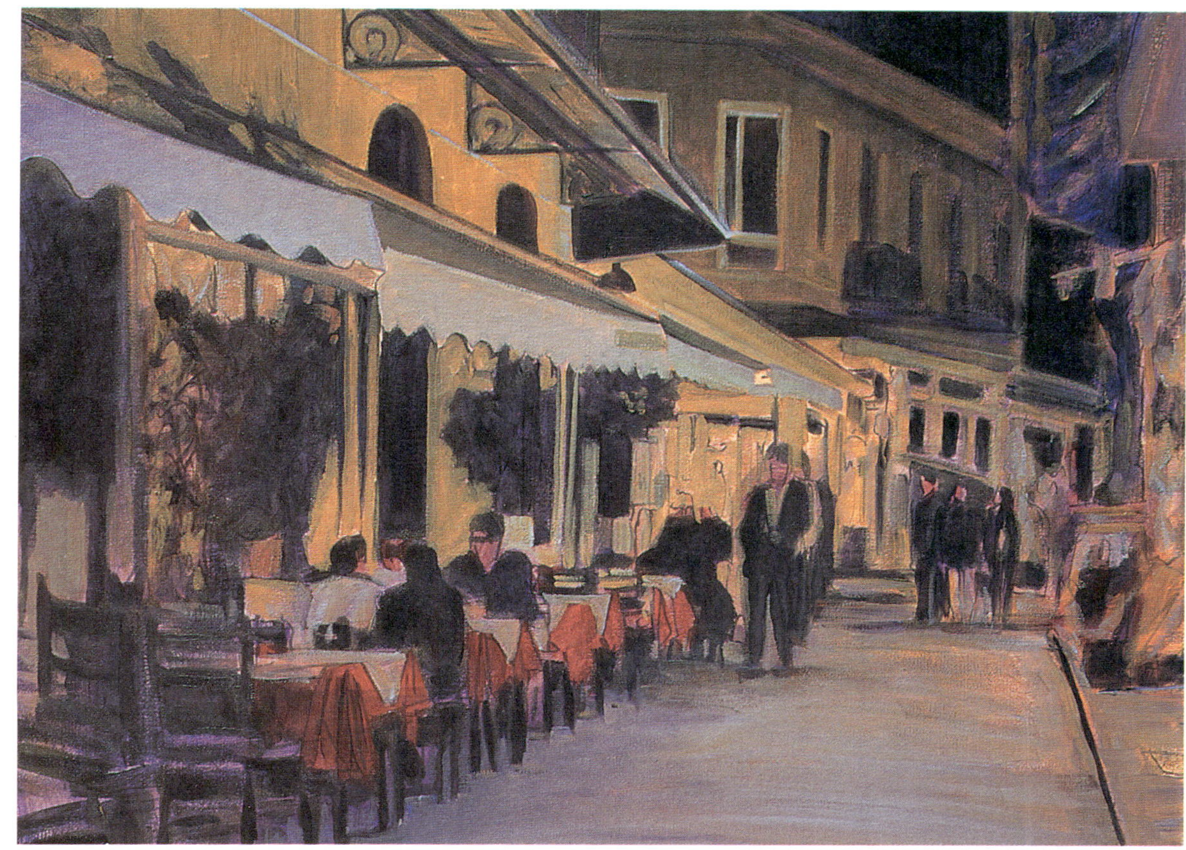

5 Next I bring up the mid-range values, starting with the distant buildings and a mix of raw sienna, Payne's gray, and gel medium. I gradually lighten the color in the remaining buildings by adding yellow oxide to the mix. Next I apply a mix of light blue-violet, yellow oxide, and light portrait pink to the awnings, table-cloths, and figures. I add the same colors to the street and a few abstract shapes on the right, some-times lightening the colors by incorporating some un-bleached titanium.

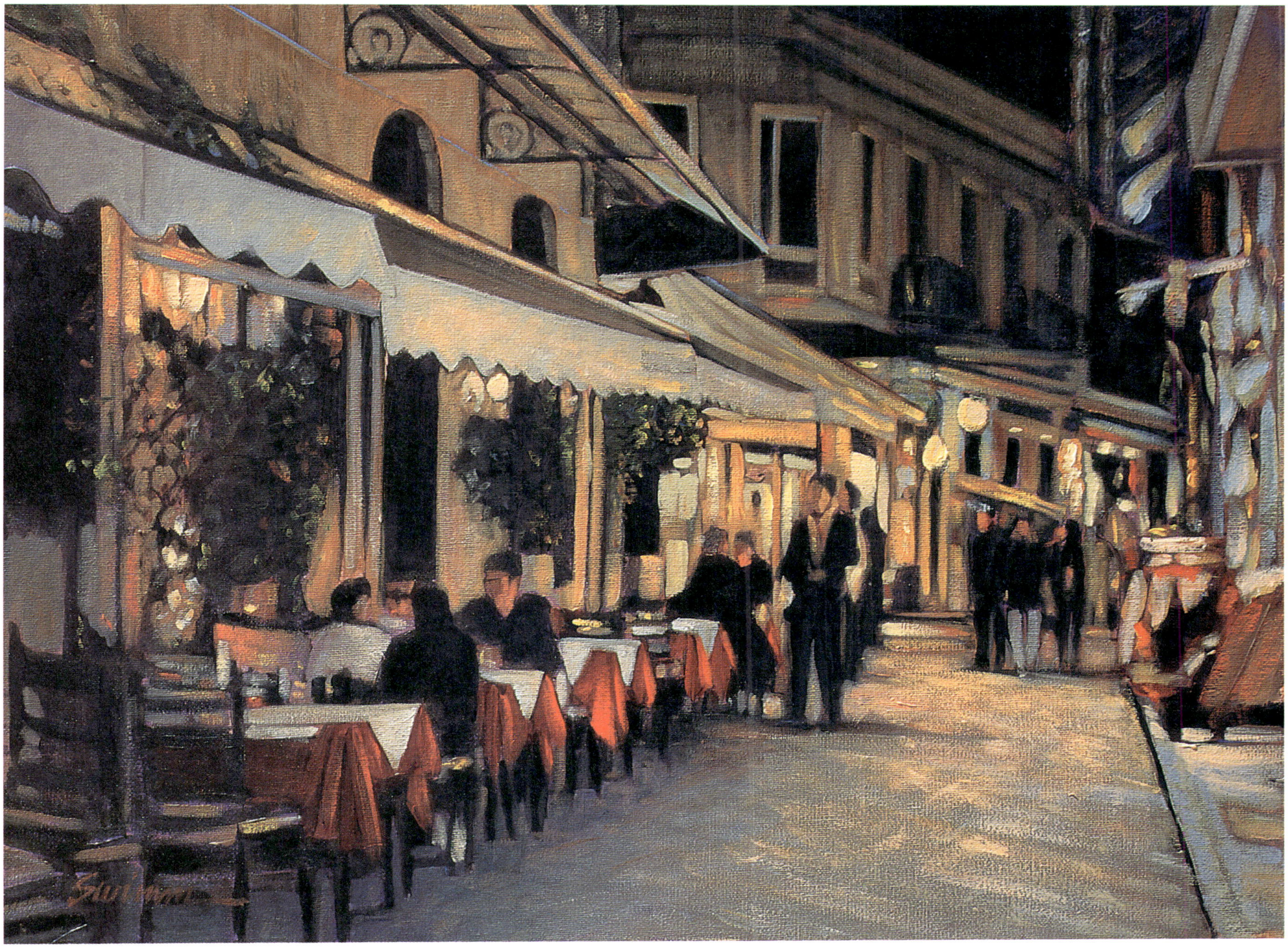

6 With a thicker, more opaque mixture of paint, I further define and embellish the shapes and details. Using a large flat brush, I add accents to the buildings, awnings, and win-dows. When the paint dries, I develop the details with drybrush, scumbling medium-free paint onto the surface to create texture. This works especially well in the walls of the build-ings and the street. Next I add the lightest highlights, applying light blues, pinks, yellows, and oranges with both thick spot applications and drybrush strokes. Then I build up another layer of color in the street, mixing gel medium with the paint for spots of solid color. I also add final touches to the figures, the foliage, and the buildings.

CONTRASTING VALUES

The eye is naturally drawn toward light values, so objects painted with lighter colors seem to "pop" forward in a scene. It's possible to take advantage of subtle contrasts between light and shadow (see "Exploring Light and Shadow" on page 10), but a more dramatic pairing of contrasting elements—such as very light colors against a dark background—can further intensify the effect. For this scene in coastal Stresa, Italy, I chose a colorful, sunlit building façade as my focal point. The building would attract the eye against nearly any colored backdrop; but the dark values of the neighboring buildings and shadowed street provide a particularly striking contrast, immediately establishing the center of interest.

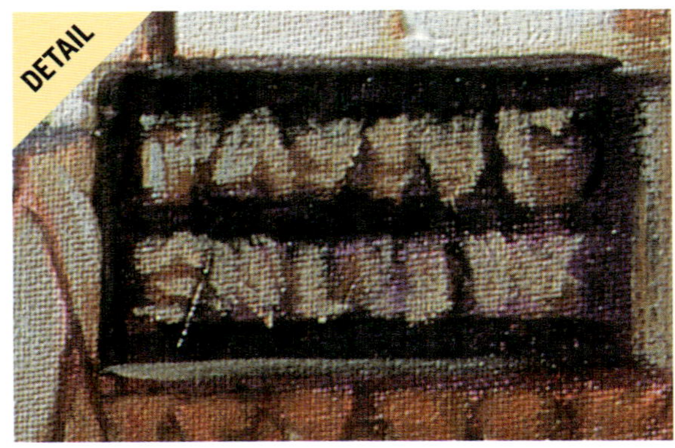

PRODUCING LETTERING There's no need to meticulously reproduce signs with great detail—I prefer to give the impression of lettering rather than replicating it perfectly. For this sign, I use quick strokes, giving enough detail to establish the sign without rendering it exactly.

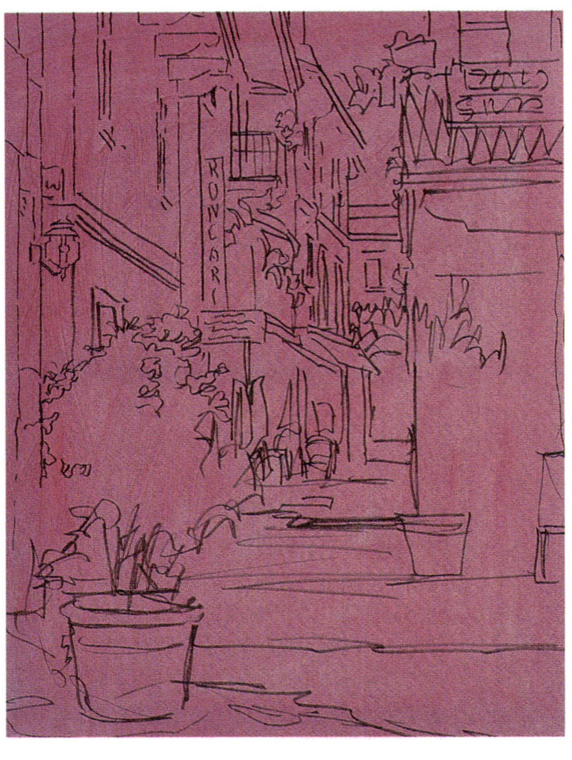

1 I start depicting this street scene with a rough sketch on my canvas. After drawing the major visual elements with a fine-line marker, I cover the entire canvas with a thin wash of medium magenta. This underpainting will add warmth and harmony to the finished painting.

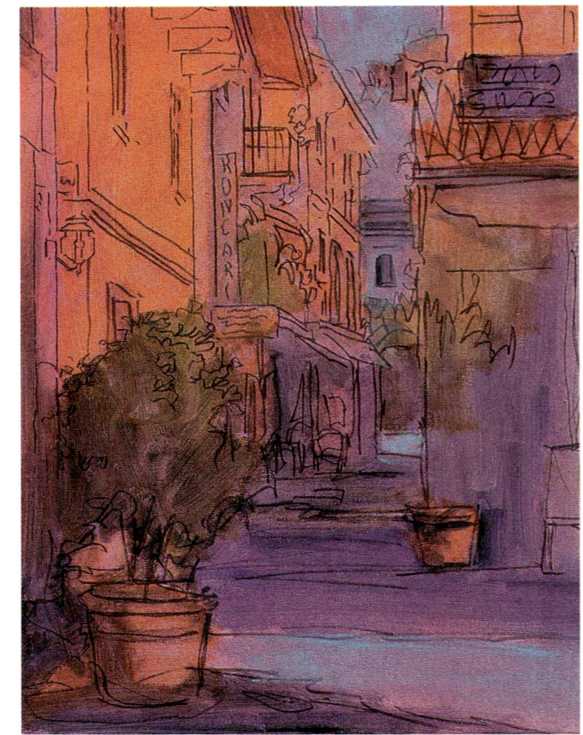

2 When my underpainting is dry, I block in the largest areas of color using a large flat bristle brush. At this stage, I keep the paint transparent so that the drawing is still visible. I also mix the colors—dioxazine purple, Payne's gray, sap green, burnt sienna, raw sienna, and light blue—with gloss medium before applying them to the canvas.

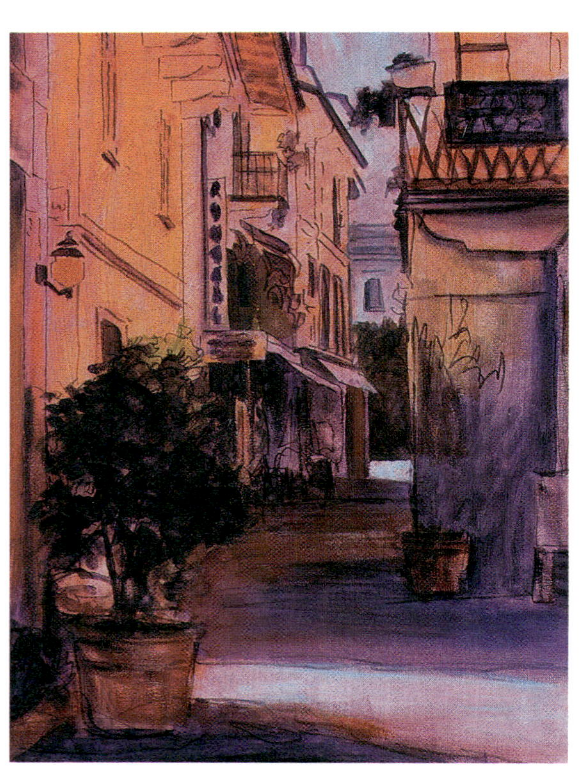

3 Now I focus on defining the darkest areas of the scene. Using the edge of my brush, I add shape and architectural details to the buildings. Then, with a mix of sap green and Payne's gray, I apply shadows to the foliage. I also mix dioxazine purple with burnt sienna for shadows in the street. Although the painting is still at a beginning stage, the contrasts between light and dark are already beginning to reveal themselves.

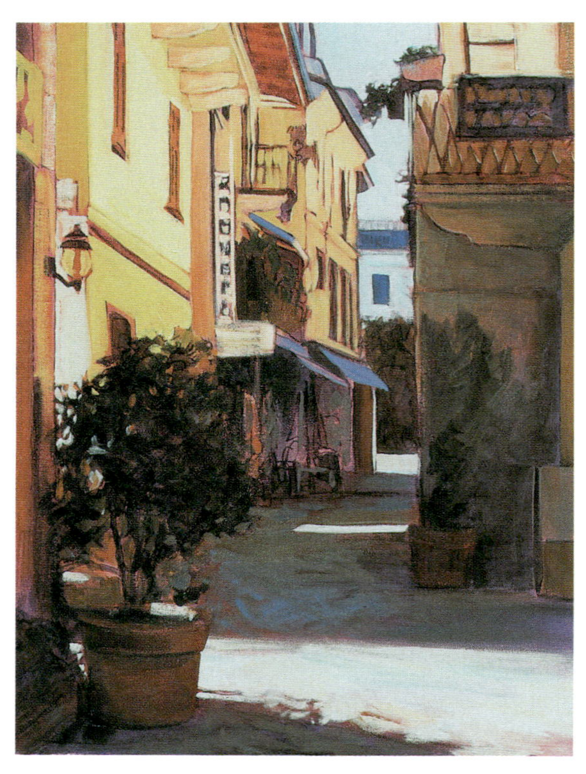

4 Next I fill in large areas of highlights with various mixes of red oxide, yellow oxide, light portrait pink, unbleached titanium, and light blue-violet, mixing in gel medium for opacity. I start with the buildings on the left and then continue with the remaining buildings, the sky, and the street. Next I use sap green mixed with light blue-violet to define the leaves of the foreground plants, switching to burnt sienna mixed with Payne's gray for the planters. I also touch up street and building shadows using various mixes of light blue, dioxazine purple, burnt sienna, unbleached titanium, red oxide, sap green, and Payne's gray. (See color samples on page 27.)

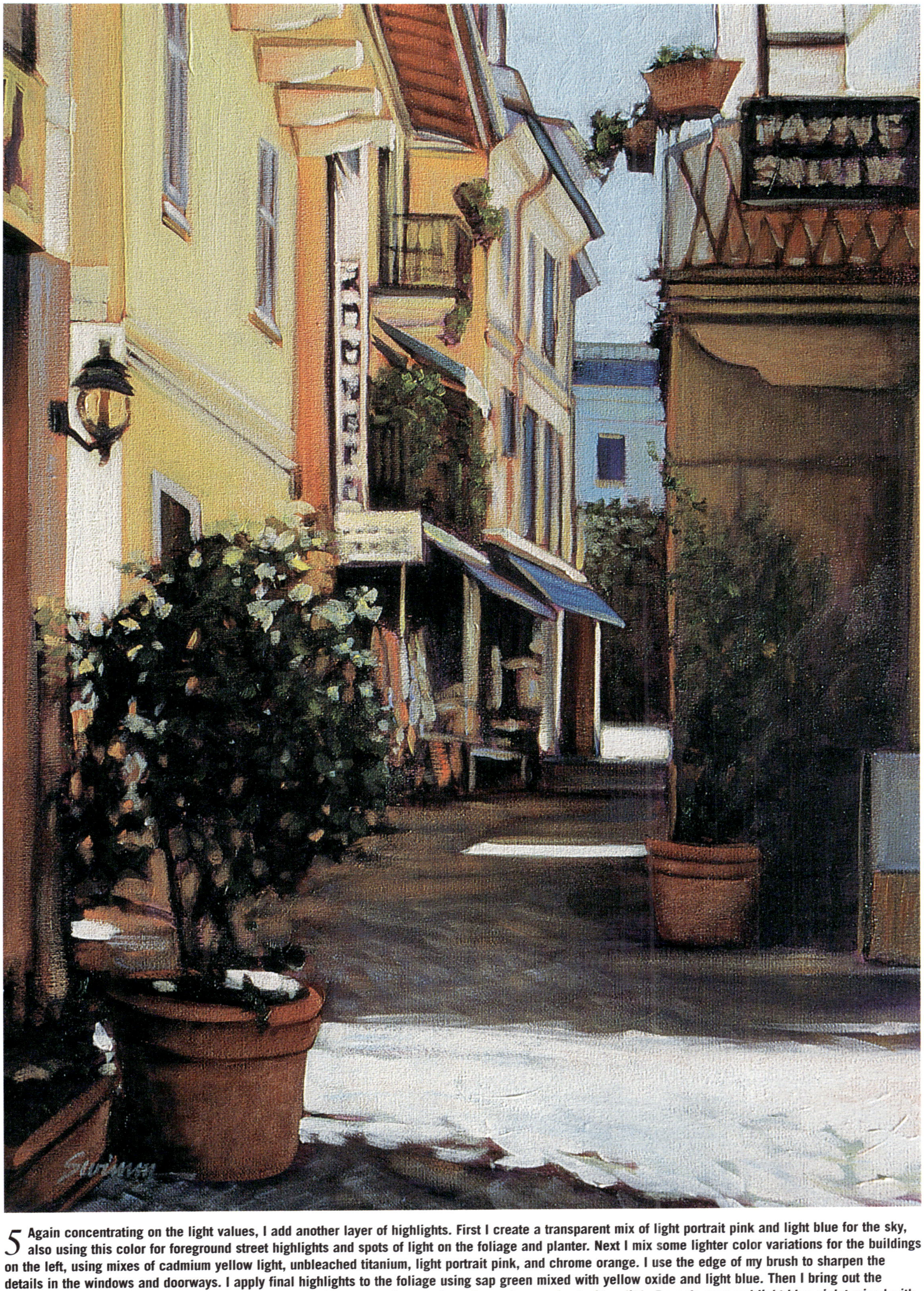

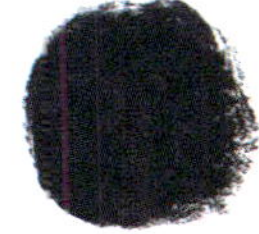

Dioxazine purple +
Payne's gray

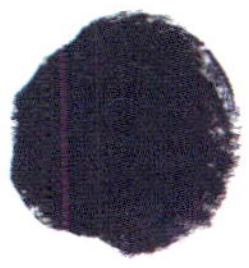

Dioxazine purple +
light blue

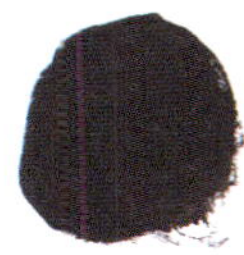

Dioxazine purple +
burnt sienna

Sap green +
Payne's gray

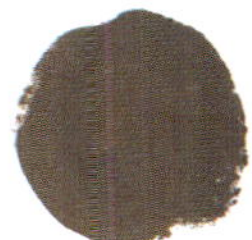

Unbleached titanium +
red oxide

5 Again concentrating on the light values, I add another layer of highlights. First I create a transparent mix of light portrait pink and light blue for the sky, also using this color for foreground street highlights and spots of light on the foliage and planter. Next I mix some lighter color variations for the buildings on the left, using mixes of cadmium yellow light, unbleached titanium, light portrait pink, and chrome orange. I use the edge of my brush to sharpen the details in the windows and doorways. I apply final highlights to the foliage using sap green mixed with yellow oxide and light blue. Then I bring out the reflections in the shadow areas of the street by drybrushing on random strokes of raw sienna mixed with a little Payne's gray and light blue-violet mixed with a little Payne's gray. I also use drybrush to soften edges, including the horizontal edge of the foreground shadow. To finish, I add one more layer of highlights to the planters, this time using red oxide mixed with Payne's gray.

TELLING A STORY WITH A FIGURE

Street scenes can take on an entirely new life with the simple addition of a human figure. In paintings, figures speak through their body language, which can relay a range of emotions to the viewer, such as relaxation, tension, or excitement. In painting, this nonverbal speech is called "gesture." *Gesture* typically refers to a movement of the body that expresses or emphasizes ideas or feelings, but gesture can also animate a part of the body, such as a finger or an eyebrow. In this painting of Tuscany, Italy, the figure has a slightly stooped posture, shuffling gait, and wearily raised arm that produce a sense of exhaustion—conveying dismay at the long road ahead.

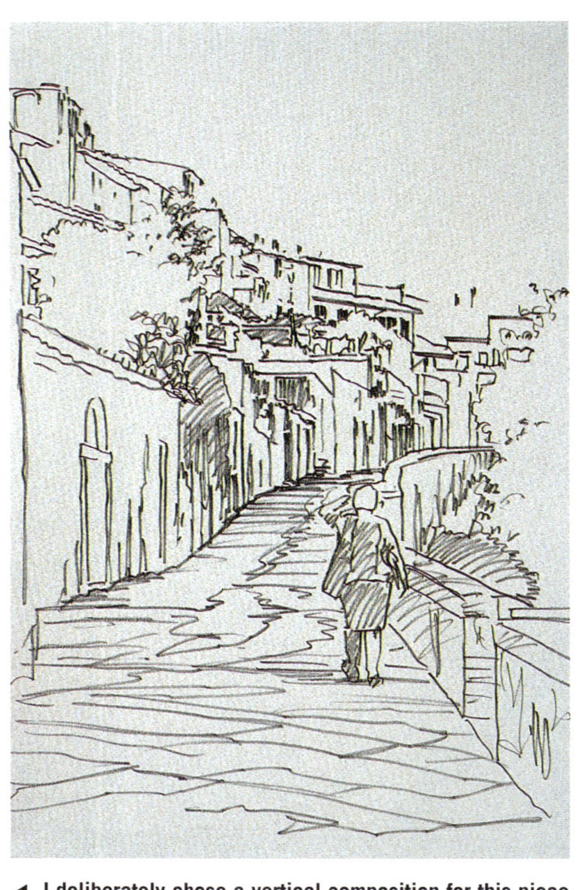

1 I deliberately chose a vertical composition for this piece to showcase the steep hill and the compact, overlapping buildings. After choosing the format, I make a rough sketch of the scene on a 36" x 24" canvas with a fine-line marker, mapping out the basic shapes and shading.

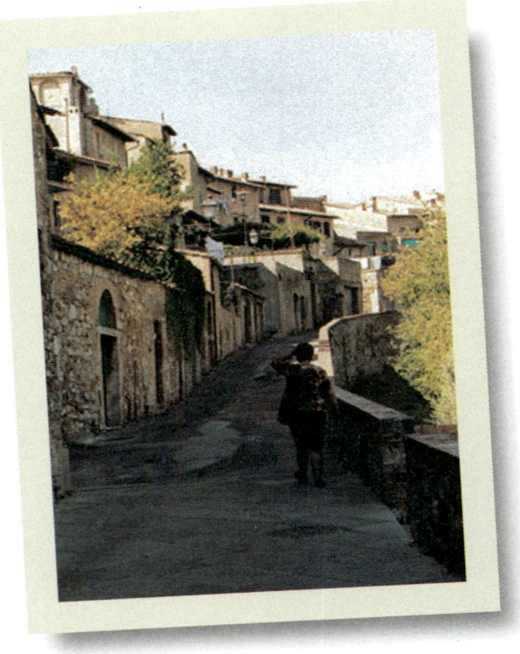

INCLUDING A FIGURE I had a variety of photos of this scenic town, but I selected this one to paint because of the woman walking up the pathway. Including her figure made the composition more interesting than just showing the buildings alone, as it seemed to add a bit more "story" to the painting.

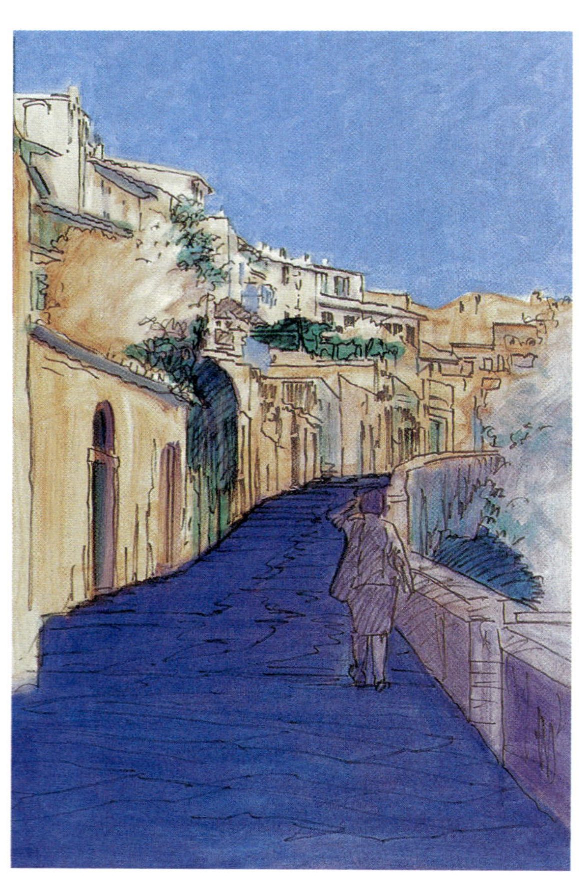

2 I mix gloss into my paints and apply burnt sienna to the buildings; Prussian blue to the street; light blue-violet to the sky; Prussian blue mixed with phthalo green to the foliage; and dioxazine purple to the figure, wall, and shadows.

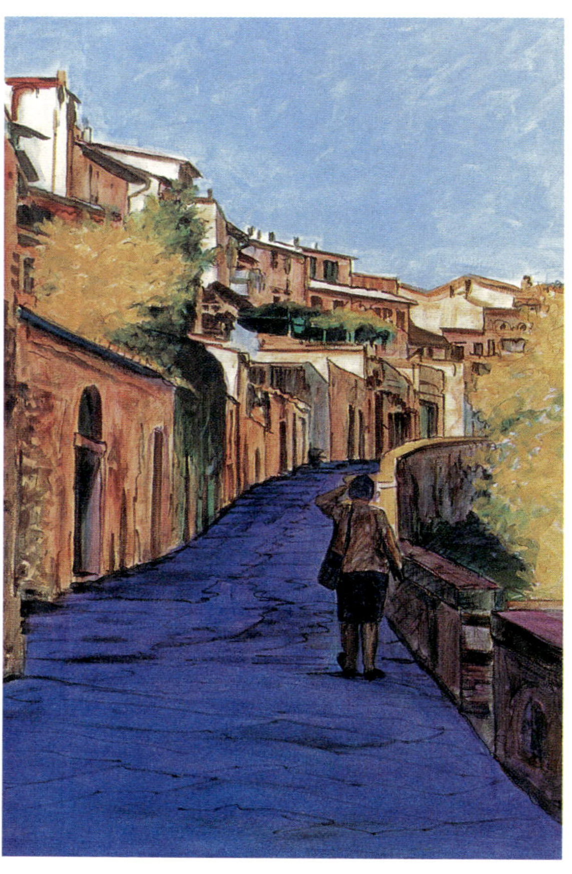

3 I apply a mix of Prussian blue, Payne's gray, and burnt sienna to the figure, wall, and roofs; and sap green mixed with Payne's gray to the foliage. I glaze the street with a purple and blue mix, using burnt sienna for the buildings.

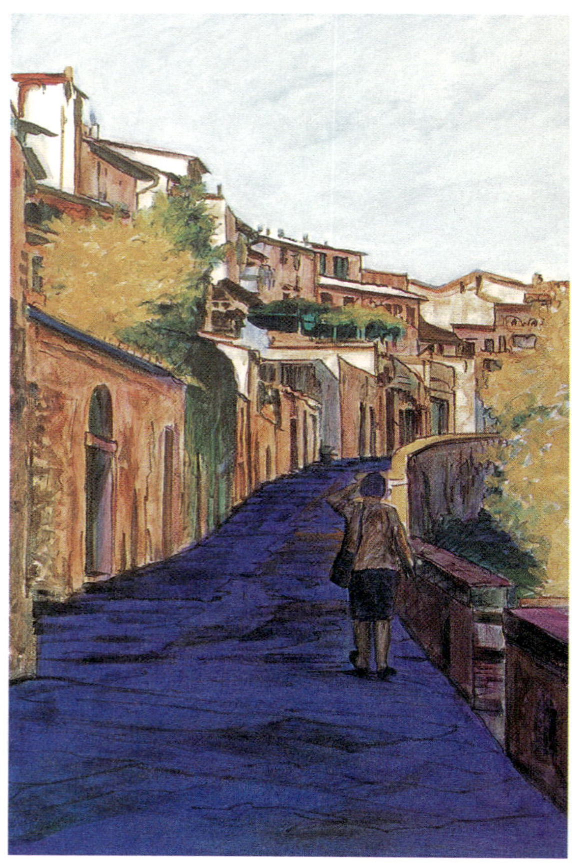

4 Now I apply raw sienna to the foliage. I glaze magenta over the building shadows and a mix of Payne's gray and phthalo green over the street, adding burnt sienna highlights. Over the sky, I glaze unbleached titanium mixed with gloss.

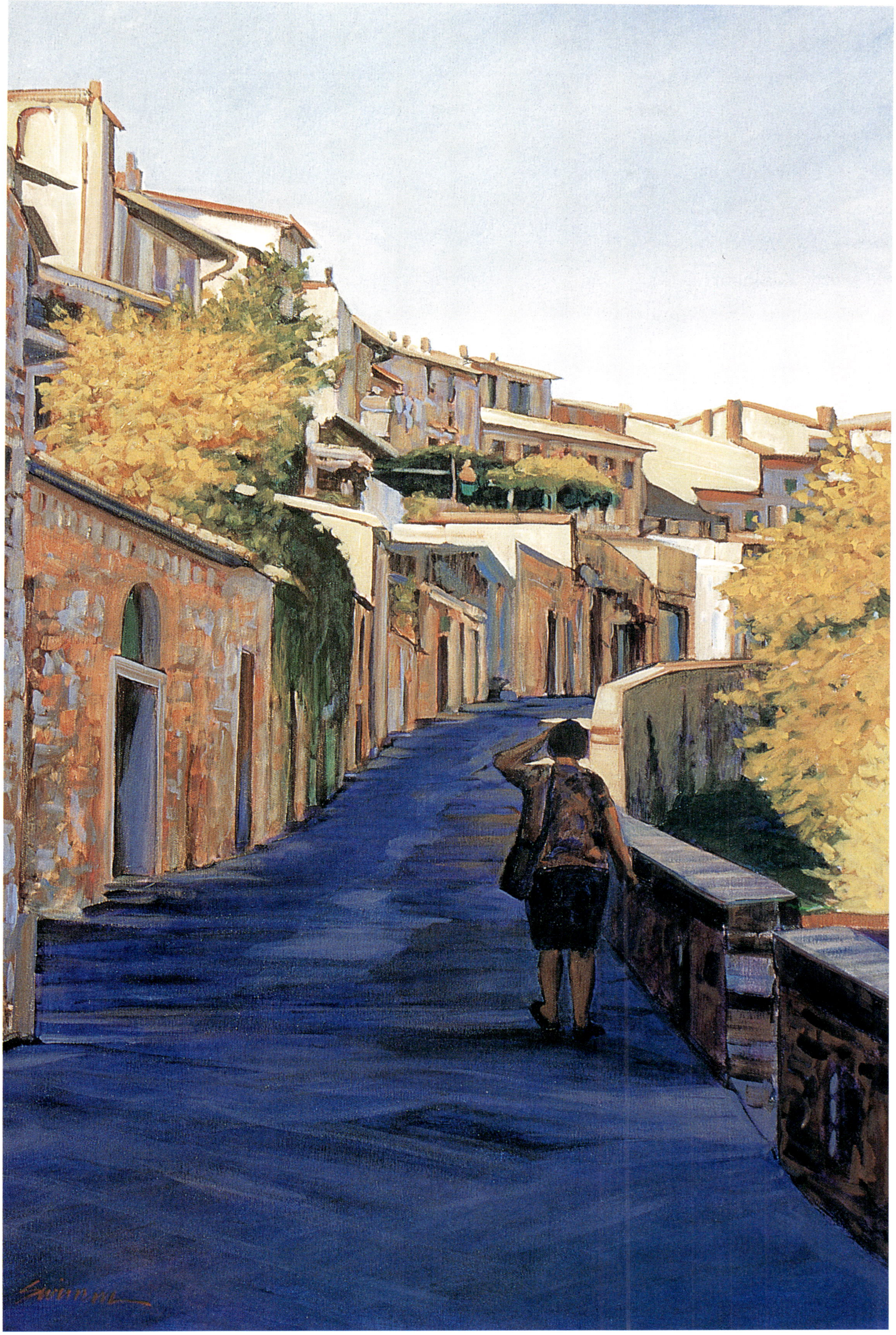

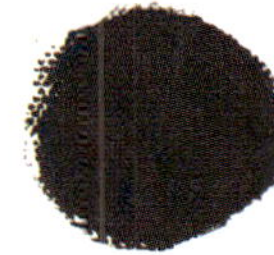

*Payne's gray +
light blue-violet*

*Payne's gray +
light blue-violet +
Prussian blue*

*Red oxide +
Payne's gray*

5 For the street's finishing touches, I mix three colors (see color samples), thin the paint with gloss, apply it with crisscross strokes, and blend while it's still wet. Next I dab light blue-violet mixed with burnt sienna and raw sienna onto the buildings for texture. Then I apply burnt sienna mixed with dioxazine purple and light blue-violet to the figure. To brighten the sky, I apply a mix of light portrait pink and light blue-violet, blending as I work from top to bottom. I highlight the trees with a mix of raw sienna, yellow oxide, and sap green. Then I highlight the buildings with thick mixes of red oxide, white, and cadmium yellow medium.

SEEING COLOR IN WHITES

There's more to working with whites than simply cracking open a tube of titanium white. In a painting, white is definitely not the absence of color; rather, it is often filled with reflections of the colors that surround it. Tint your whites to reflect the other colors in the scene, as I did by including the delicate colors of the sea and sunset in the whites of this breathtaking scene in Santorini, Greece.

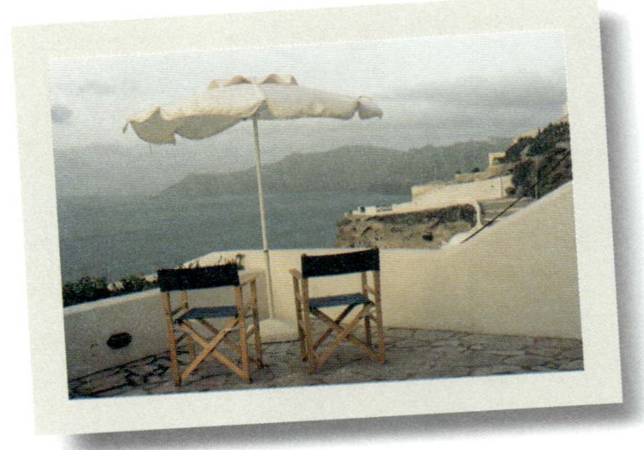

◄ **EXAGGERATING REFLECTED COLOR** In this photo, you can see a few nuanced colors reflected in the white umbrella and the off-white wall. But to emphasize the reflected color and add drama to the scene, I'm going to change the time of day, pulling in sunset colors and reflections.

OPAQUE COLORS

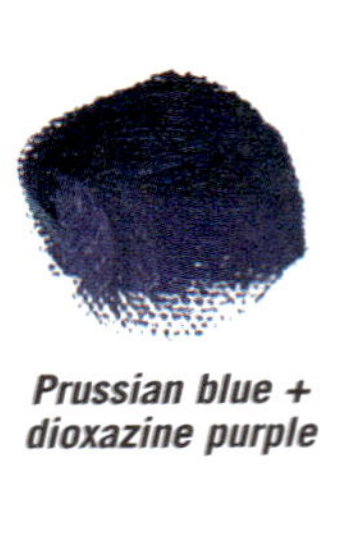

Prussian blue + dioxazine purple

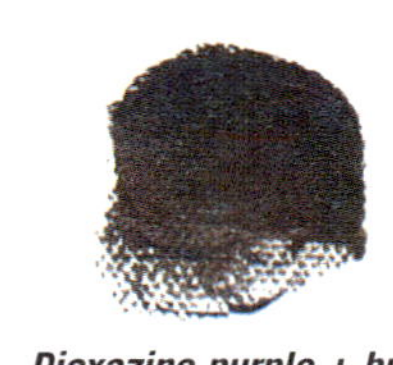

Sap green + cerulean blue

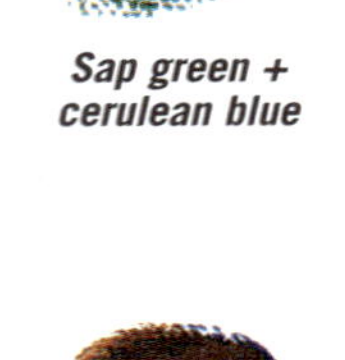

Dioxazine purple + burnt sienna + unbleached titanium

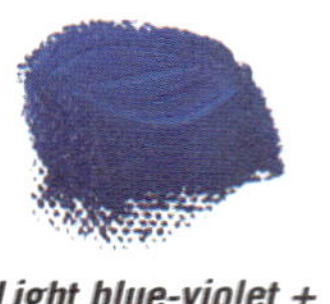

Light blue-violet + dioxazine purple

Magenta + burnt sienna

Dioxazine purple + burnt sienna + Payne's gray

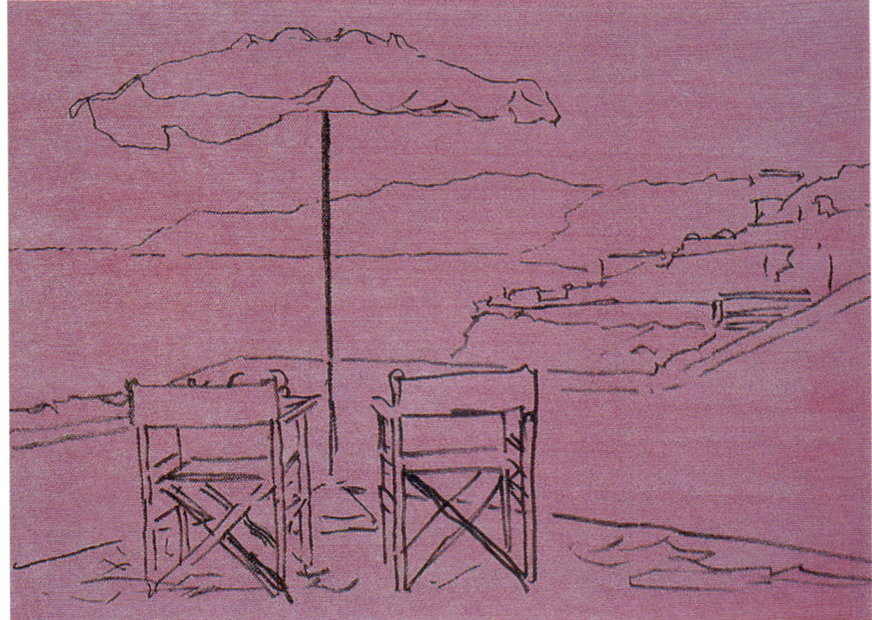

1 Using a small 12" x 16" canvas, I make a rough sketch that defines only the most important shapes and areas of color separation. Then I wash over the sketch with a thin, transparent wash of magenta, which will enhance the warmer tones of the painting as well as help to unify and harmonize later applications of color.

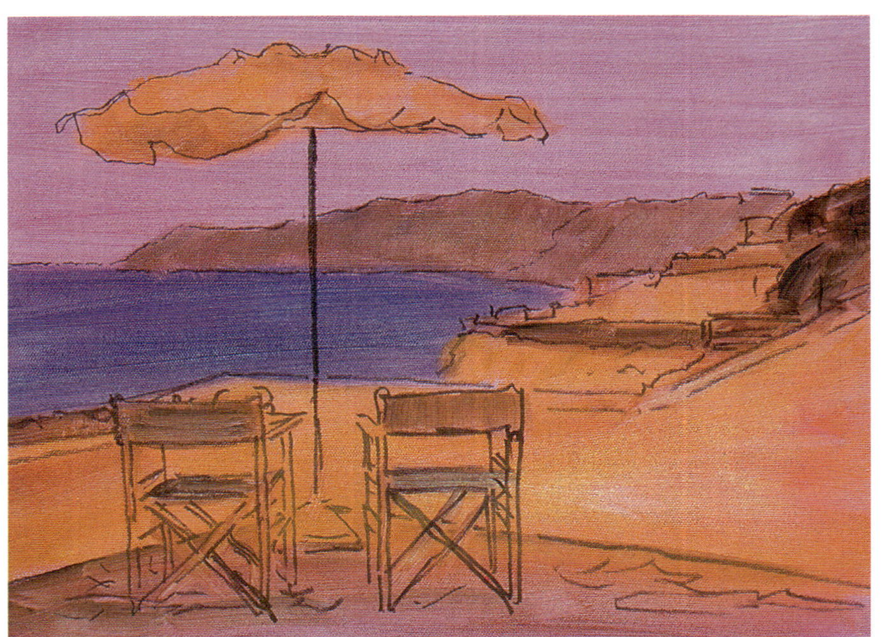

2 I mix dioxazine purple with burnt sienna, adding gloss medium to improve the flow of the paints; then I rough in the hills and water with this mixture and a medium flat sable brush. Next I switch to raw sienna for the umbrella and the walls—again adding gloss medium to the paints—and I mix in sap green, Payne's gray, and dioxazine purple for the darkest areas of the foliage and chairs.

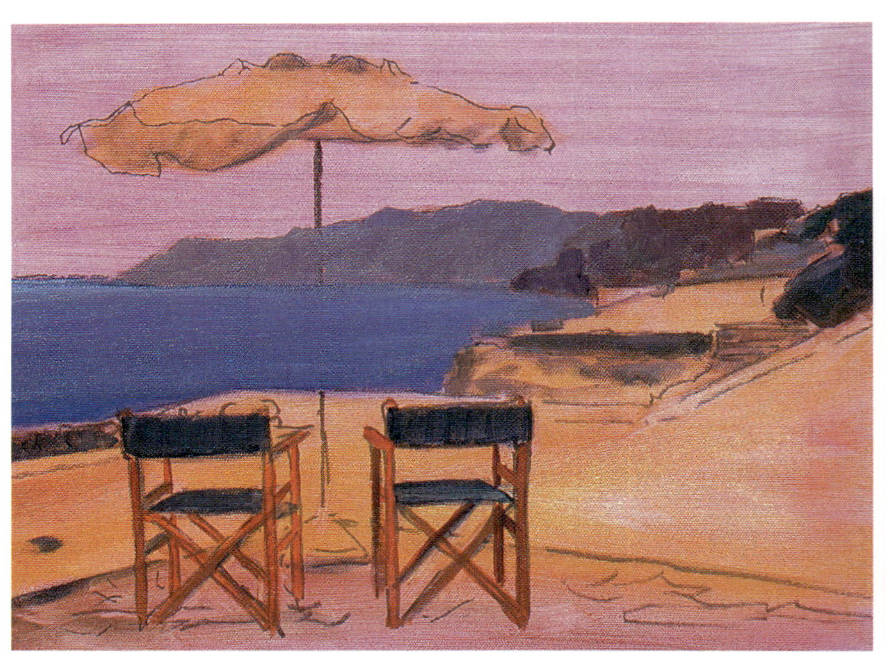

3 Next I apply more opaque color (see color samples), adding a light-blue mix to the background hills and moving forward with a purple mix. Then I apply a thin layer of Prussian blue to the water, blending in cerulean blue and light blue-violet while it's wet. I use a darker blue mix for the deck chairs and shadows; then I switch to sap green mixed with cerulean blue for foliage. I add details to the chair legs with a mix of magenta and burnt sienna.

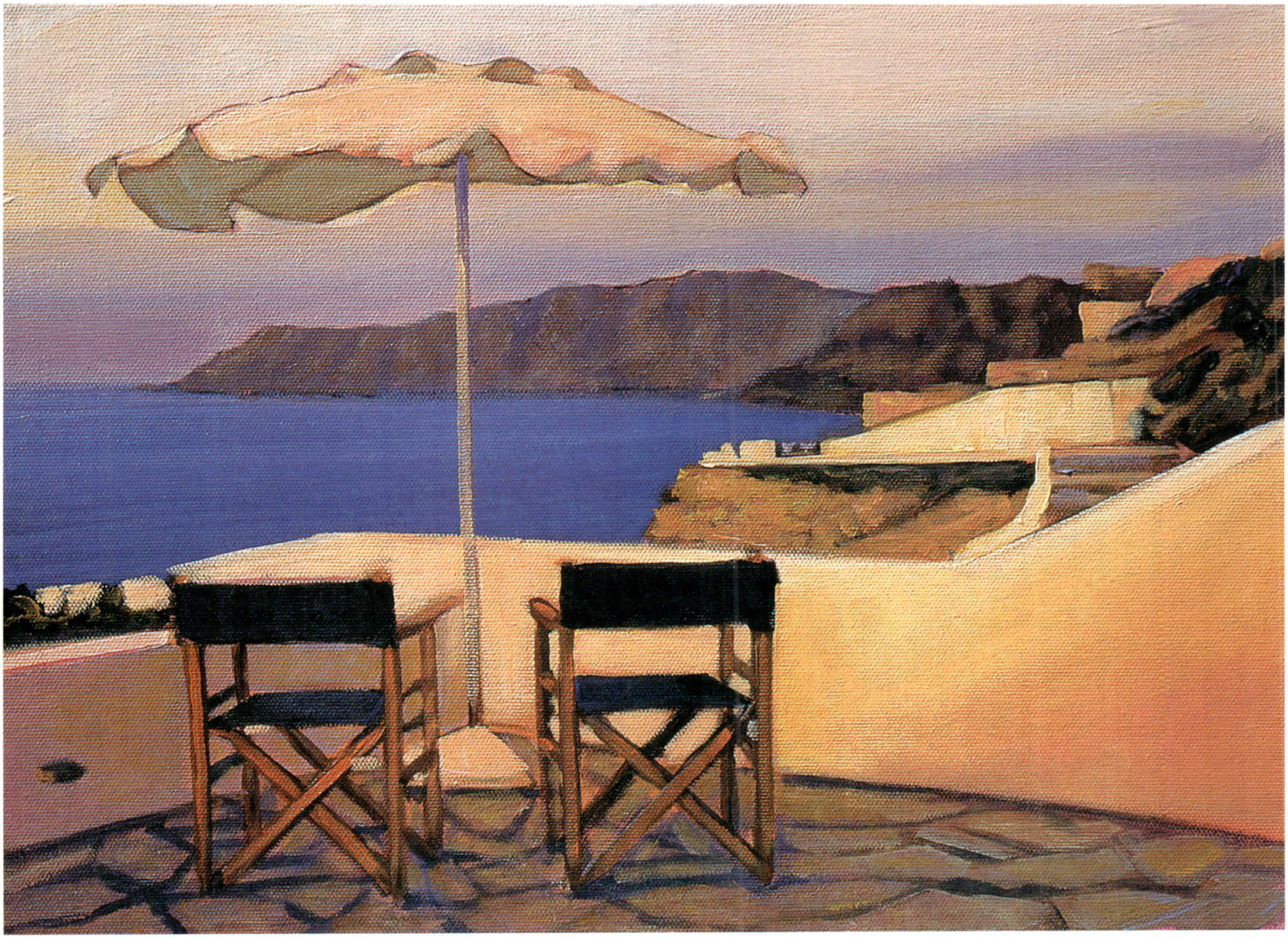

6 To complete the painting, I make a few final value adjustments. First I build up the highlight colors of the wall by applying reflected colors from the sky—yellow oxide, light
portrait pink, and magenta. Then I add details to the chair arms and legs with burnt sienna.
Using leftover mixes from the palette, I adjust a few colors in the shadows. Then I add one
more layer of color to the patio, filling in the areas between the outlines and highlighting
the pole using unbleached titanium, which I mix with a little touch of dioxazine purple in the
shadow. Note that it's not just the white umbrella that reflects the colors of the setting sun
and surrounding ocean—even the stucco walls, patio tiles, and chair frames do.

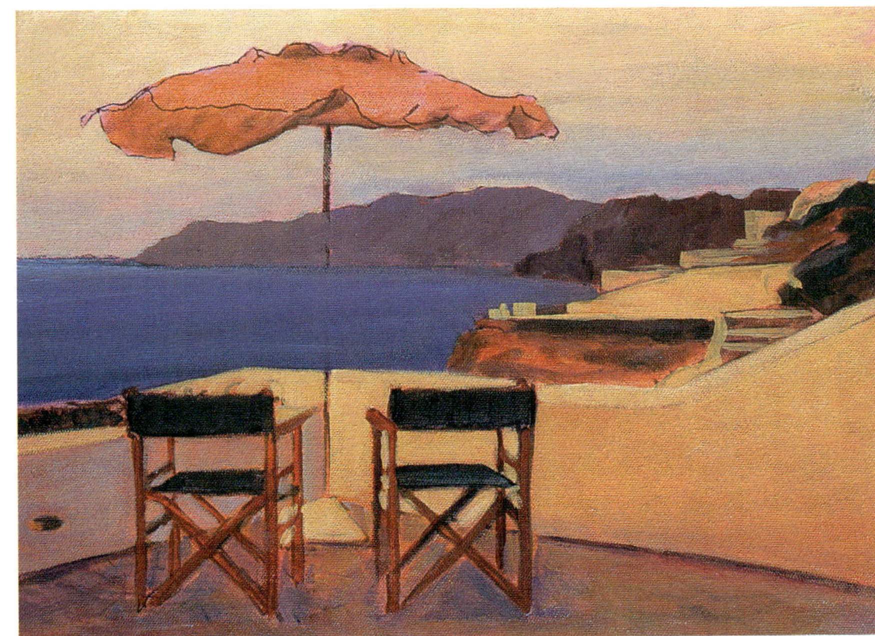

4 Now I work into the sky with light portrait pink, yellow oxide, and magenta—thinned
with gloss medium—blending the colors from top to bottom. I add a little light blue-
violet as I get closer to the horizon. Using the same mix, I add reflected color to the walls.
Then I darken the shadows in the foreground with dioxazine purple, magenta, Prussian blue,
and raw sienna, suggesting the tiles. Then I add light blue-violet to the wall.

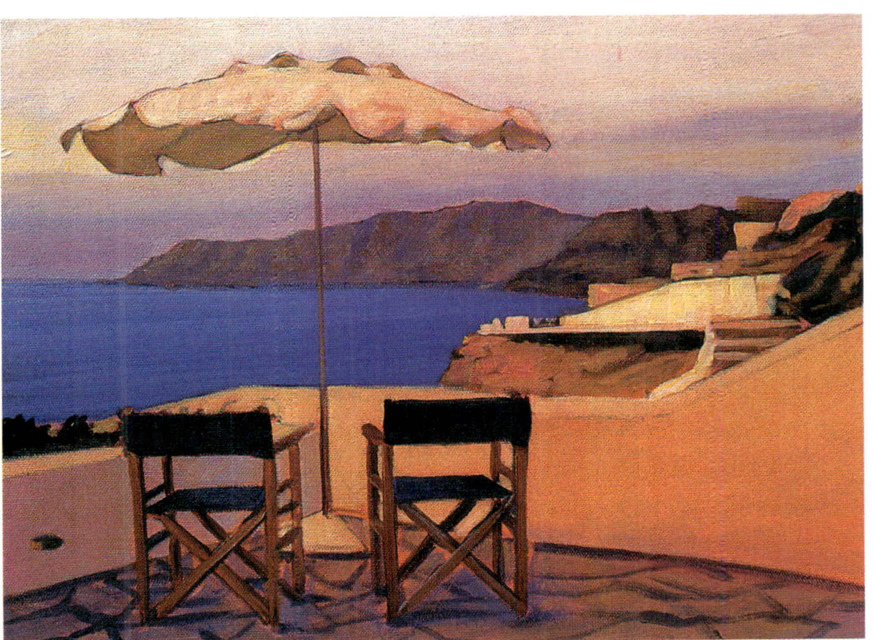

5 With a mix of burnt sienna, light blue-violet, magenta, and bronze yellow, I add color to
the hills. I add another layer to the water, blending as I move from top to bottom. And I use
Prussian blue to darken the chair fabric and patio tile outlines. I also add another layer of sky
color, lightening with unbleached titanium. I apply the sky color to the umbrella too; for shadows, I mix raw sienna with Payne's gray. For wall highlights, I mix Naples yellow with white.

Walter Foster Art Instruction Program

THREE EASY STEPS TO LEARNING ART

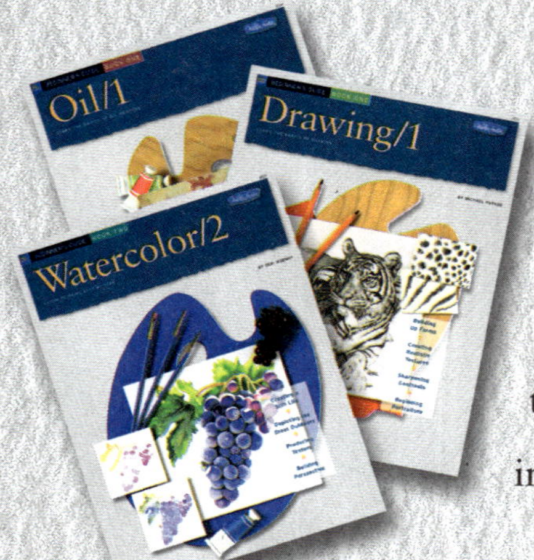

Beginner's Guides are specially written to encourage and motivate aspiring artists. This series introduces the various painting and drawing media—acrylic, oil, pastel, pencil, and watercolor—making it the perfect starting point for beginners. Book One introduces the medium, showing some of its diverse possibilities through beautiful rendered examples and simple explanations, and Book Two instructs with a set of engaging art lessons that follow an easy step-by-step approach.

How to Draw and Paint titles contain progressive visual demonstrations, expert advice, and simple written explanations that assist novice artists through the next stages of learning. In this series, professional artists tap into their experience to walk the reader through the artistic process step by step, from preparation work and preliminary sketches to special techniques and final details. Organized by medium, these books provide insight into an array of subjects.

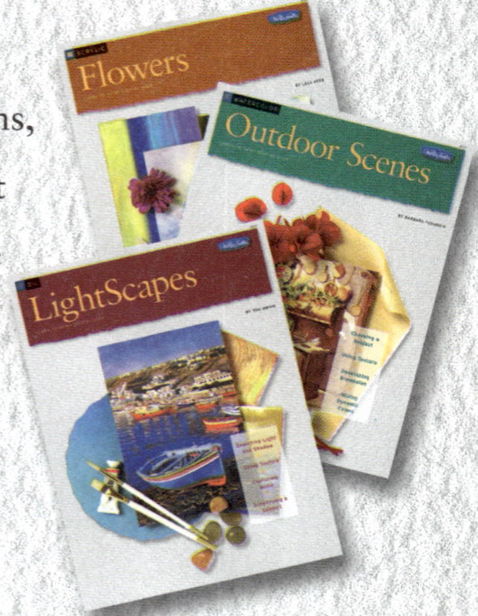

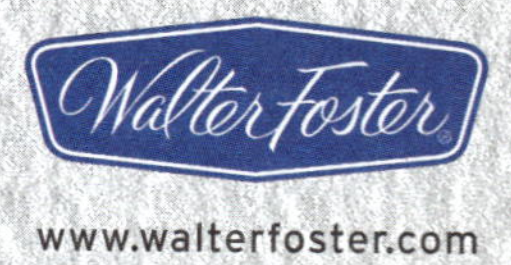

Artist's Library titles offer both beginning and advanced artists the opportunity to expand their creativity, conquer technical obstacles, and explore new media. Written and illustrated by professional artists, the books in this series are ideal for anyone aspiring to reach a new level of expertise. They'll serve as useful tools that artists of all skill levels can refer to again and again.

Walter Foster products are available at art and craft stores everywhere.
For a full list of Walter Foster's titles, visit our website at www.walterfoster.com
or send $5 for a catalog and a $5-off coupon.

WALTER FOSTER PUBLISHING, INC.
23062 La Cadena Drive
Laguna Hills, California 92653
Main Line 949/380-7510
Toll Free 800/426-0099

www.walterfoster.com